'5

D0551292

A PRACTICAL GUIDE TO
PRIZE-WINNING PHOTOGRAPHY

David Davenport ARPS

The Oxford Illustrated Press

© David Davenport, 1987

Printed In England by J.H. Haynes & Co Limited,
Sparkford, Nr Yeovil, Somerset

ISBN 0 946609 46 2

Published by:
The Oxford Illustrated Press, Sparkford, Nr Yeovil
Somerset BA22 7JJ

Haynes Publications Inc, 861 Lawrence Drive,
Newbury Park, California 91320

British Library Cataloguing in Publication Data

Library of Congress Catalog Card Number

Contents

Foreword

It has been my pleasure to be associated with camera clubs for over thirty years and in that time I have observed the enthusiasm and striving of the keen amateur photographer, but so often one hears the plea: "I would love to go in for competitions but I do not feel I am up to that standard—are there any books published that would help me?"

Here then is very good news for prospective competitors and who better than David Davenport to produce such an informative publication.

David is the voice of experience. I have followed with much interest his numerous achievements in the world of competition, his close attention to the judge's comments and his untiring efforts to succeed.

Prize-Winning Photography is a mine of valuable information gained from personal experience and fulfils a long awaited need amongst photographers.

Hubert Thompson, ARPS, APAGB

The Way To Success

Every year, superb prizes of goods, cash and luxury holidays are among the breathtaking inducements-- offered in photographic competitions which are promoted and sponsored by manufacturers, organizations, photographic magazines and the press. The contests present an exciting challenge to the keen photographer. You too, can enjoy the fun and sense of anticipation when you enter a contest and derive further pleasure from a stimulating aspect of an absorbing hobby.

An Exciting Challenge

The elation of receiving an award and the thrill of having a picture published also engenders a feeling of achievement. So often the newcomer to photography assumes that there is little chance of success when competing against experienced photographers who possess elaborate equipment, yet this is not so. Be assured that it is unnecessary to own sophisticated apparatus in order to produce a prize-winning shot. What is required is a camera with a lens capable of reproducing sharp images, and some knowledge of what constitutes a good photograph.

Whether you are an established enthusiast or a keen beginner there is a contest for you to enter. Someone has to win, so why not you?

The Standard Required

In competitions run by photographic magazines, the judges consider technical competence as well as subject matter, but in other contests, particularly those with a holiday theme, it is often originality or the humorous content of the picture which is the deciding factor, and on those points everyone stands a chance.

'Brothers': To the onlooker, the two dark-clothed figures were anonymous, yet as they walked together the similarity of shapes and shadows characterized an affinity. I had already observed the two men earlier but had been unable to get an unobstructed view. Then they appeared again giving me opportunity to picture them against a diagonal setting from an elevated viewpoint.
  The winner of a supreme award in a camera club exhibition.

OM-1   Kodachrome 64   75-150mm zoom   1/125th sec @ f11

In photographic clubs it is not uncommon for a newcomer to obtain an award over more experienced members because of a different approach and an uninhibited style. In a similar way a fresh approach could also win an open contest, but it should be noted that competitions held nationally usually attract a vast number of entries and it is only after drastic sorting and elimination that the eventual winners emerge.

A competition entry should show a good technical standard in addition to the ingredient of originality. To achieve recognition be ultra critical of your own work. Eliminate any prints which barely conform to the theme of the competition and never enter anything that is badly lit or devoid of interest. The winning pictures are likely to be published, which means they must be sharp, display a good range of tones and reveal detail in the shadow areas, so print quality is an important factor for success. Unless the image is exceptional, poor processing will relegate a picture to the reject pile.

Although the majority of camera users are more concerned with the finished result rather than deliberating on technicalities, provided the limitations of the equipment are observed, most cameras will produce satisfactory pictures for photographic contests. Your success is also related to the type of competition; if the categories announced are not your strong point then go in for contests which do appeal to you and submit the subjects you are best at producing.

Contests which are organized by the provincial or national press occasionally extend over a few months and include weekly or monthly awards during the period of the competition. The interim winning pictures are usually published and often give an indication of the style of photography which is favoured.

Originality

If the contest is an annual one, reference to previous results can be enlightening, but never attempt to duplicate ideas of past winners, as similar pictures are unlikely to win an award. Study former prize-winners by all means, but avoid copying their style. Consider them only as a guide to forming another approach based on your individual interpretation of the theme. Try to anticipate the sort of picture required then aim at subject matter which is imaginative and artistically pleasing. Although you may consider that the winning entries of some contests are mediocre, never let that be the reason for submitting commonplace prints yourself.

A competition can give a sense of purpose to your photography. When you enter a contest you are in effect participating in an assignment, seeking to portray a subject in an original way and producing an entry within the time limit set for the contest. By testing your creativeness and technique against other enthusiasts you are acquiring experience which, even if you fail to reach the awards list, will be beneficial for future contests.

Your opportunity for success depends on leaving nothing to chance, The fact you are competing means you are trying to attract attention to your picture, so your subject matter and presentation must be strong enough to impress the judge that your submission is the most outstanding photograph in the contest.

Planning Your Approach

When a competition is announced that is the time to think about your approach and to make a note of all your ideas. You can either search through your existing negatives or transparencies to assess whether any are appropriate to the categories or, better still, plan to take some photographs specifically for the contest. This, of course, would be necesssary if the rules stated that pictures had to be taken within a particular period. Occasionally an original idea will come to mind straightaway, but more probably, inspiration for an imaginative picture will only evolve through careful consideration and after you have dismissed the more obvious ideas which many others will have thought of too.

Every effort to take good photographs is commendable and necessary if you are contending with other enthusiasts, but the exciting spark of inventiveness in your interpretation of the theme is all important in your striving to win.

There is always a great sense of achievement when you are successful with a photograph which you planned and produced specifically for a contest. As you cultivate your approach to picture making with contests in mind, it will also boost your competitive spirit. Maintain a high standard by being critical of your own work to the point of being ruthless with anything which falls short of the best.

The very suggestion of entering a competition immediately creates an incentive for improving your photography. Not merely from the thought of winning a prize, it also sets a target for personal achievement. The knowledge that your photographs are competing against the work of others is a spur to attaining a better standard.

Being involved in a competition assignment is more than just an exercise. In your efforts to produce a photograph of prize-winning quality you also gain valuable experience. As you seek to capture lighting variations, exaggerate perspective, or emphasize texture, each operation activates your skill towards the objective of composing a picture creatively and presenting the subject matter in an original manner.

Contest Classifications

Each year hundreds of contests are run by newspapers, periodicals and various companies, so always be on the look-out for details of new competitions

'Quiet Break': A lot of satisfaction was derived from capturing this picture from between parked cars and passing pedestrians in Washington D.C. The colour, line and form of the architecture was the subject matter that had attracted my attention. While waiting for an appropriate gap in the bustling activity, the pipe-smoking man in uniform settled down in front of the structure—in the right place as far as competition judges have been concerned. With the benefit of a zoom lens, I was able to frame the subject as tightly as possible, eliminating the unwanted distractions without having to change the camera position.

A commended award in the Rushden Open Colour Slide Exhibition was followed by an acceptance in the Nottingham National Open Exhibition of Photography and a trophy for the best transparency in a club Annual Exhibition.

OM-1   Kodachrome 64   75-150mm zoom   1/125th sec @ f5.6

which can be found in displayed advertisements, editorials, obscure paragraphs, leaflets, or in the most unexpected places such as on the backs of food cartons and chocolate wrappers. Make a note of those which interest you, observing the theme, the kind of pictures required, the various sections or categories, and the closing date. As a general guide, photographic competitions can be divided into the following classifications:

Group 1: Manufacturers, Newspapers, General

Magazines: Contests which are promoted by manufacturers and the press offer substantial prizes and, consequently, attract an enormous entry. Quite often these competitions seek the happy-snapshot type of photograph which depicts children, animals or family activity, where the appeal of the subject matter is the important factor. It is in this section that the inexperienced photographer can compete, with a good chance of winning a prize. The contest with a holiday theme is found in this group and the

Left: 'Precious Moment': An example of a picture in the family snapshot category which can succeed in attracting the judging panel's attention by its simplicity and charm. The first time it was submitted to a competition it was awarded first prize of an Ilford Sportsman 35mm camera in a local newspaper contest. Further recognition followed in *Good Photography* magazine and *Photo News Weekly.* Over 20 years had elapsed since the first win, when I entered the shot for a 'Recall Your Tender Moments' competition organised by Birds Eye Foods, the details being made known on the company's food wrappers. Usually, only recent photographs are entered for contests, and when rules stipulate this, one should always observe the condition. However, my reason for sending in a picture from the past was that the picture should have captured (a) A special moment in your child's life (b) A day always to be remembered or (c) An unexpected visit. The idea was that if you did not have a snap readily available, you looked through your album to find an apt entry. Within a few weeks a letter arrived informing me that 'Precious Moment' had won a £500 travel voucher and a complete home movie outfit.

Bessa 1   Ilford FP3   1/125th sec @ f16   Illuminated by flash

popularity of the subject is reflected in the thousands of photographs these competitions receive.

Group 2: Local and Travel Organizations. Specialist Magazines: Prizes are not always as large as in the first group but the number of entries is proportionately smaller. Nevertheless, well-produced prints always stand a better chance of success.

Never be haphazard in choosing your picture and refrain from submitting anything which is substandard. Among the subjects for this category are those pertaining to the interest of the organization or magazine, which provides scope for imaginative subject interpretation of a hobby or interest.

Group 3: Photographic Publications and Photographic Manufacturers: Competitions in this group are often for a set subject with emphasis on technique, composition and print quality. The winning pictures are usually reproduced. The aim of photographic publications is to entertain and also increase the knowledge of their readers. It should be recognized that a considerable proportion of subscribers to any photographic journal are experienced and proficient photographers, competition is intense and print quality is of a very high standard. Those seeking experience at this level of competition are recommended to, first of all, enter any beginners' contests which are sometimes included in magazines. Also in this category are the manufacturers of photographic materials and equipment, who promote

Opposite page, top: 'Corbiere': Photographs are occasionally referred to as being of a picture postcard style, usually because the print in question is more of a record shot of a landscape than one which displays creative flair. However, picture postcards should not be considered in such a disparaging manner, because many suppliers maintain a very high standard of photography. The shot of Corbiere does come into the record category, with foreground rock formation providing some framing. The photograph is one example of subject matter that travel organizations seek when they sponsor competitions.

Runner-up prize in the Jersey Tourism Photographic Competition.

Exa 500   Ektachrome   50mm lens   1/125th sec @ f5.6

'Tug-o-War': For these contests the action is usually confined within a predictable area which greatly assists pre-focusing. I have observed that pictures of the entire team are not always so effective as shots of two or three of the contestants exerting their strength. I took this shot at a moment when the two teams were equal to each other in effort and the rope was almost motionless.

An award winner of film to the value of £50 and a certificate in the Amateur Photographer of the Year competition and selected for the AP/Kodak exhibition at Hamiltons Gallery, London.

OM-1   Kodachrome 64   75-150mm zoom   1/125th sec @ f5.6.

competitions, often in conjunction with a national magazine. Usually a condition of entry is that the manufacturer's materials must be used in the production of any picture submitted.

Group 4: Exhibitions: The privilege and satisfaction in having your pictures displayed with the work of experienced photographers, and the prestige derived from any subsequent publicity, are the rewards for your work being accepted for exhibition. Sticker labels for the reverse side of the prints are awarded for each picture hung. Sometimes trophies or cash prizes for the best pictures in the show and certificates or special awards for the runners-up are also given. Although both large and small prints are accepted by the majority of exhibitions these days, this group is for the enthusiast and advanced photographer who owns or has access to processing and enlarging facilities and can produce up to 20″ x 16″ (50.8 x 40.6cm) mounted photographs. A number of exhibitions include sections for transparencies.

Study The Rules

The first thing to do when you are attracted to a competition is to study the rules carefully. If they clearly state a maximum and minimum print size, then keep strictly to the conditions of entry. Occasionally organizers request the negatives of winning pictures, so do not enter a contest with that sort of clause if you are not willing to part with the negative. From time to time you will come across rules which stipulate that the copyright of winning photographs or transparencies will be transferred to the organizers. Very substantial prizes could make it worthwhile, but this sort of condition should be treated with caution. It is better to keep clear of contests where the transfer of copyright is one of the rules.

There are also competition rules which state that although the copyright remains with the photographer, the print or transparency may be used for publicity in connection with the contest. Although that is quite reasonable, be wary of the rule which allows the promoters to use a picture for *any* purpose.

Competitions to Ignore

Generally, competitions are well organized and fairly run, but once in a while a contest is advertised which appears to have been arranged solely for the purpose of the sponsors obtaining pictures for nothing. One such contest required the copyright of all pictures to be assigned to the organizers and stated that any photograph submitted should not have been published elsewhere. An entry fee was also required.

A competition which has a clause in the rules which allows the sponsors to retain non-prizewinning entries for their own use and without payment, should

also be avoided. Any picture that is considered to be worth using is also worthy of being recognized in some way, such as in some contests conducted by the photographic press, when the rules state that although prints will not be returned, photographs of merit will be retained and filed for possible future publication for which the photographer would receive a reproduction fee.

A most important rule in contests refers to the last date for the acceptance of entries. It is in your own interest to ensure that your pictures are despatched well in advance of the deadline. If you are anxious about a very special print or transparency arriving safely, you should use the recorded delivery service.

In some competitions, the rules are published only as a brief outline in an advertisement or magazine feature. If you consider the information to be insufficient, you should try to obtain full details by applying to the organizers.

The following list contains rules which are typical of those issued for the average competition. To submit an entry implies acceptance of the published conditions which usually indicate:

1. The type of subject required.
2. The number of photographs each entrant may submit.
3. The number of categories, and whether they are beginners or advanced sections.
4. Whether black-and-white or colour prints, or transparencies may be submitted.
5. The maximum and minimum size of photographs permitted.
6. Whether an entrance fee or a competition coupon is required with each entry.
7. Any technical details which must be included—the type of film used, shutter speed and aperture setting.
8. That the photographer must be the owner of the copyright. (Sometimes it is stated that any print submitted must be the entire work of the entrant.)
9. Entering the competition implies permission for the photograph to be published.
10. Occasionally, it is stated that the prints must not have been published or have won prizes elsewhere.
11. All entries to be accompanied by a stamped and addressed envelope or packaging for return of prints.
12. The last date for receiving entries.
13. No correspondence to be entered into regarding the competition.
14. No photographs accepted without a completed entry form.
15. The photographer's name and address to be written on or attached to each print or transparency.
16. Only photographs taken during a specified period are eligible.

17. No responsibility is accepted for damage to or loss of photographs or transparencies.

18. The competition is for bona fide amateur photographers who do not make more than 10 per cent of their living as a photographer.

It is possible to read the rules with care and then unwittingly break one of them. An entrant in a national competition was disqualified after being adjudged the winner because he had inadvertently included a picture which was ruled to have been taken outside the period stipulated. The prize was very special indeed—a new car, with accessories and fully taxed. It was offered for the best portfolio of transparencies suitable for a calendar and the photography had to be carried out during the months from June to December.

The result was eventually announced in the *Amateur Photographer* magazine and the winning pictures published. From the printed evidence the photographs were well worthy of the award, but, in a subsequent issue of the magazine it was stated with regret that the portfolio had been disqualified and the prize awarded to another photographer. It was reported that the decision had not been taken lightly and was made only after legal advice had been sought.

The reason given was that one of the transparencies in the original winning portfolio was a duplicate of a slide taken about two years before the competition had been announced, therefore it had not been photographed in the period laid down in the rules. Although the duplicate was made within the specified competition period, the disqualification was unavoidable because the duplicate was considered to be a copy or a reproduction of an original in the same way a print is produced from an original negative.

The majority of competitions are impartially run, and entrants should contribute to the goodwill and spirit of the contest by observing the rules. If it is stated that prints which have gained awards in other contests are ineligible, then ensure that you comply with the conditions. Always abide by the rules because your success could depend on it.

Pleasing The Judges

In national competitions it is customary for the names of the judging panel to be known when the contest is first advertised. In these larger events the panel will probably include a celebrity in the person of a well-known photographer or an editor of a photographic magazine.

Among the hundreds of entries to be considered

'Hilltop People': A strong cloud formation provides a pleasant backdrop for an unusual silhouette frieze which maintains a lively interest throughout its span. This is due to the continuity of the iron fence and the variety of positions assumed by the figures in silhouette.

An award winner in a camera club exhibition.

OM-1   Kodachrome 64   50mm lens   1/250th sec @ f5.6.

there will be a proportion displaying a good standard of photography plus those which are above average, and where the photographer has been able to inject additional appeal into the picture. It might be an unusual viewpoint, an arresting expression, dramatic lighting or eye-catching impact that will cause the judging panel to take a second look and evaluate its merits. Naturally, judges have their prejudices, and such differences are sometimes apparent in their final assessment. One adjudicator will prefer a certain style whereas a colleague may dislike it.

For some of the larger competitions which are organized annually, the judging panel comprises the same members each year. If the panel remains consistent, the style it favours should be apparent. Such preferences do not have as much bearing in competitions as in exhibitions when before a print can be in contention for an award, the first requirement is for the picture to be accepted by a selection committee.

When an exhibition is announced, the members of the selection and judging panel are usually made known too. To the experienced exhibitor the names are sometimes familiar as also are the panel's inclinations.

Although it is necessary to please the judges if you want to have your talents acknowledged, do not let this fact inhibit your style or prevent you from entering an imaginative picture because it might be rejected on the basis of being unconventional.

On the matters of quality and technical consideration, most judges will have similar thoughts. It is on the points of subject interest, interpretation and picture appeal that opinions differ. It is unlikely that you will satisfy everyone with your style, choice of subject or picture arrangement, but you should ensure that any pictures submitted will not lose points for faults such as an over-exposed transparency or a poorly printed photograph.

One of the benefits of camera club membership is obtained during competition evenings when you can listen to a qualified judge evaluating your photographs. To actually hear for yourself a judge's personal opinion is more profitable than merely receiving a rejection slip through your letter box and can be invaluable to improving the quality of your pictures.

Always be prepared to have your work criticised as well as praised, but never be discouraged by adverse remarks. Prints which win acclaim in national contests do not necessarily achieve success in club competitions. Also because a print has won awards at club level it does not follow that it will obtain a prize in a contest organized by a magazine.

Judges who include constructive criticism in their appraisal are to be preferred to those who seek to say something pleasing about every print on display. Although no one is offended, not much is gained when the only indication of a judge's preferences is

'Harvest Field': A straightforward shot has achieved success for a number of reasons, none of which is outstanding, but each has contributed to the overall appeal of the picture. A high viewpoint has given a perspective that a position from ground level would not have revealed. Also from the higher level the low light can be appreciated with its effect on the uneven lines, which are clearly defined. The bales and the tractor lead the eye around the picture which is dominated by a variety of green hues.

'Harvest Field' was selected for *Camera Weekly* magazine's Readers' Pictures feature. Although it is not run as a competition, payment is made for all photographs that are published.

OM-1   Ektachrome 64   75-150mm zoom   1/125th sec @ f8

when the awards are announced. Unfortunately such assessment is of little significance to entrants of pictures which are below standard. The judges who are always appreciated, especially by the beginner, are those who clarify their criticism in a kind and helpful manner.

In club circles, the photographer soon becomes aware of the likes and dislikes of certain judges who, from time to time, come in for a fair amount of criticism themselves. However, it should not be forgotten that they are volunteers, who devote a lot of time to judging club competitions and sometimes receive very little appreciation for their efforts.

Benefits of Club Membership

Participation in club competitions and exhibitions allows you to compare your prints with those of other members.

One of the pathways towards success is receiving guidance and suggestions from fellow photographers. Every opportunity to view your work through the eyes of someone else can be educational and a worthwhile exercise in your striving for success. Sharing a common interest and comparing ideas can also be extremely informative.

In addition to furthering your interest in competitions, belonging to a photographic club or society enables you to hear lecturers who are expert in the many aspects of photography and permits you to attend practical demonstrations, studio groups, and enjoy club outings to places of photographic interest. Some clubs have the additional benefits of a library or darkroom facilities, and the majority hold an annual exhibition which usually reveals the high quality of photography which can be acheived.

There are a number of excellent photographic magazines which encourage and involve the photographer who is a keen competitor. As well as sponsoring numerous contests, the magazines provide up-to-date information on cameras and equipment, publish outstanding portfolios and instructive articles, and are illustrated by well-selected pictures.

Dealing with Rejection

When a competition entry is unsuccessful, never dismiss the photograph as a failure but try to analyse why it did not succeed. First of all was the picture suitable for the theme? Did the print have sufficient appeal or impact to arrest the attention of the judging panel? An entry must be able to withstand scrutiny in a number of aspects, for although a picture may have impact it also requires good technique and needs to be presented imaginatively.

Critically re-examine the composition, lighting, subject matter and viewpoint. If you feel your picture was beyond such scrutiny, then you must consider

'Williamsburg Carpenter': One disadvantage of photography on holiday is that if any shots are not as successful as you had hoped, there is little to be done to remedy the fault. The shot of the carpenter is an example of this. Although favourably received by camera club judges, it is unlikely to achieve any major prizes on account of the man's face being in shadow. It is now a simple matter to suggest a fill-in flash would have lightened the shadows. Anyway, the picture is a reminder that one should always consider and re-consider the subject that is before the camera. So often, an apparently insignificant detail can cause a picture to lose marks in a contest.

A camera club award winner.

OM-1   Kodachrome 64   50mm lens   1/125th sec @ f5.6

whether the shot was not the kind the judges were looking for, or if it was entered in the wrong category. Sometimes another opinion will suggest faults or lack of appeal which have not been apparent in your personal appraisal. If, after reflection, you still think the photograph has sufficient merit, plan to submit it to another suitable contest.

One way of overcoming the feeling of discouragement when you have been pipped at the post, is to have another contest result to look forward to. After you have sent a picture to a competition do not sit back and wait for the result before competing again, but try to maintain a competitive spirit and enter other contests, so that if one photograph is rejected there is always another print somewhere to carry your hopes.

When seeking to succeed you should remember that for every winner there are many losers. So be prepared for the time you too will experience the taste of defeat when your prints are returned with a stark rejection slip.

Prizes

Cameras, enlargers, projectors, flashguns and lenses are but a few of the dazzling items of equipment which are presented to the winners of photographic contests. Cheques, travel vouchers, holidays abroad, inscribed cups, medals and plaques are further examples of the numerous prizes that are to be won.

As competition categories differ, so does the value of the awards offered. In one contest, which was announced as one of Britain's richest, the array of prizes amounted to £10,500. In another competition, the prize for the winning transparency was £5,000—a very large sum for just one picture.

An unusual yet exciting first prize was a £30,000 house offered in a contest run jointly by a soap powder maufacturer and a building company. 13,000 people entered the contest in which they had to submit a photograph depicting a magic moment, accompanied by a caption of no more than 15 words. In the conditions the organizers stated that they were not looking for the best quality photograph but rather the imaginative skill of the photographer in capturing the moment, together with the most apt and relevant description of why the picture was 'magic' to the entrant. Such an award is exceptional, but there are many other contests which offer splendid and worthwhile prizes not only for the first place but for the runner-up positions too.

In some competitions an additional pleasure is for the winners to be invited to a presentation luncheon, where they can meet the judges, photographic journalists or the editor of the magazine involved in the organizing of the contest. Often there is the bonus of seeing your photographs in print when the results are published.

Entering competitions is a fascinating way of

'Young Lad': An informal portrait, photographed by bright available light from a window, with a sheet of white card to reflect light into the shadows. The hat, often worn during play periods, seemed to fit the mood and go with the clothes the child was wearing. The camera was hand held which allowed me and the 'model' to move around and not be confined to one position.

Awarded a supreme prize for the best transparency in a camera club exhibition, and a runner-up in *She* magazine photographic contest.

OM-1   Kodachrome 25   50mm lens   1/30th sec @ f5.6

helping yourself to become a better photographer. Apart from winning one of the main prizes or receiving recognition as a runner-up, the fact of having your photograph selected is a reward in itself. Go ahead and accept the challenge. Each success, no matter how small, will be a fillip to making consistent progress in your photography.

Understanding Your Equipment

Today's photographer is deriving immense benefit from the far-reaching advances which have been made in the quality of modern films and equipment. The camera is no longer something associated only with holidays, but an instrument which is used for all occasions. The wide interest in photography can be witnessed in the abundance of new and second-hand equipment which is available.

Be Familiar With Your Camera

The idea that the more expensive the camera, the better the chances of winning a competition, is misleading. For a start, much depends on the way the equipment is used. Obviously, your aim should be to buy the best camera and lenses your budget will allow, but be assured that with the right handling inexpensive cameras can also win awards. A worthwhile discipline is to familiarize yourself thoroughly with every control on your camera, so that its operation becomes second nature.

During the past few years automatic cameras have arrived on the market, featuring computer technology in the form of various programmed modes, aperture and shutter priority, autofocus lenses, automatic film loading and built-in motorized film advance. The new generation of advanced cameras joins the vast array of manual models which range from those with symbols that indicate adjustment controls, to cameras with a wide choice of manually operated shutter speeds and apertures.

Apertures and Shutter Speeds

Successful pictures can be produced, provided one remains constantly aware of the adjustments to the controls which are necessary for optimum results. It is vital for cameras with a fixed shutter speed (about 1/30th of a second) to be held firmly, and for the shutter-release to be pressed smoothly. This same advice is worth following for all cameras and at all shutter speeds, as any camera movement at the moment of exposure will cause your picture to be blurred. Camera shake is a common fault which accounts for a very large percentage of spoiled pictures.

For someone who has recently obtained a camera with a full range of shutter speeds, apertures and adjustments, the values can sometimes be confusing. For the beginner it is important to remember that a higher shutter number means a faster speed. A higher 'f' number means a smaller aperture.

Camera shutter speeds are arranged so that the exposure is halved when you change to the next faster shutter speed (or doubled if you change to the next slower speed). A typical range of speeds would be indicated as: 1/30th; 1/60th; 1/125th; and 1/250th of a second. Apertures function on the same principle, the figures being marked as follows: f5.6; f8; f11; and f16. An aperture of f8 admits half the amount of light that f5.6 does, but double the light f11 allows through. For example, an exposure of 1/30th of a second at f16 allows through the same amount of light as 1/125th of a second at f8. Obviously the number of speeds and apertures vary according to the type of model and price range of the camera.

Interchangeable Lenses

Some cameras, especially the 35mm single-lens reflex models, have a wide range of interchangeable lenses available. Photographic magazines carry numerous advertisements of special offers of well-known and lesser-known makes. It has been stated that any owner of a single-lens reflex camera who uses only the standard lens, is not making the most of the instrument's versatility. Obviously, the lens is a vital component of any camera so it is wise to thoroughly familiarize yourself with the existing lens on the camera before considering an additional one.

There is always a danger of becoming encumbered with an excess of equipment. The newcomer to photography can be under the misapprehension that the more accessories and lenses that are amassed, so the photographer's ability is increased accordingly. Although it can be argued that each lens of a different focal length is ideally suited to certain subjects and locations, it is unnecessary to carry around a large number of interchangeable lenses.

The Lens for The Job

From the extensive range of lenses, the 135mm telephoto is a favourite of many photographers who use a 35mm single-lens reflex camera. It is not over large and is consequently easy to handle. Telephoto lenses have a narrower angle of view and cover a smaller area but increase the size of the subject matter. The longer the focal length of a lens, the shallower the depth of field (that is the area in which everything is acceptably sharp). The shorter the focal length, the greater the depth of field.

A telephoto lens enables the photographer to work at a greater distance from the subject than with a standard lens and this has the effect of showing apparent compression of planes. Differences in perspective will be more noticeable and distant objects will appear to be much closer to the main subject matter than they really are. It is not the focal length of a lens which alters perspective but the distance between the camera and subject which determines

'Heads Together': Having seen the possibility of a picture I moved as close as possible to capture the shot. The story of this photograph would have been lost if anyone in the group had turned towards another direction. When trying to photograph a group of people, once you have taken a shot always endeavour to improve on it with another try.

A camera club award winner.

OM-1 Kodachrome 64   75-150mm zoom   1/125th sec @ f8

the perspective in a photograph.

The 135mm lens is excellent for candid, sport and zoo photography. It is also useful for portraits, but focusing needs to be extremely accurate because of the shallow depth of field. At an aperture of f2.8 or f4, a portrait could be spoiled because of unsharp rendering of the nose or ears.

With a telephoto lens there is a greater risk of camera shake. Unless a tripod is used it is advisable to use a fast shutter speed. As a general guide you can assume that the slowest shutter speed you can confidently hand-hold will have approximately the same numerals as the focal length of the lens. For example : use 1/60th as your slowest speed for a 50mm lens, 1/125th for a 135mm lens and 1/250th

for a 200mm lens.

The 50mm lens is considered to be the standard lens for a 35mm camera and lenses of shorter focal length come into the wide-angle category. A 28mm wide-angle lens gives a very large depth of field and is suitable for architecture and landscapes, allowing a much closer approach than with a standard lens. A small spirit level can be invaluable when using a wide-angle lens for architectural subjects as it is important to keep the camera absolutely level.

A convenient alternative to using several interchangeable lenses is the zoom lens. The focal length can be varied, which enables the photographer to fill the film format with the exact image required without changing the camera position. Two popular zooms are the 70–150mm and 85–210mm.

Interchangeable lenses are also available for the larger single-lens reflex cameras which use 120 size roll film. The twin-lens reflex cameras also use the same size film and produce 6 x 6 cm negatives. Although bulky, the 6 x 6 cm models have a large focusing screen which is ideal for composing the picture and are very popular cameras.

Important advice to follow is that whatever size format you are using, always try to fill the frame with the subject. With a standard lens you can obtain changes in image size, in a similar way to using a long or short focal length lens, by decreasing or increasing camera-to-subject distance. On most occasions this would be satisfactory but it is not always physically possible to move backwards or forwards in every picture-making situation and this is where an interchangeable lens is most valuable.

Meters and Correct Exposure

Becoming familiar with your equipment extends beyond knowing your camera's controls and functions. Whichever means you employ in assessing the right exposure for your films, whether it is the camera's built-in metering system, a hand-held meter, or the recommendation of the film manufacturer's exposure guide leaflet, endeavour to thoroughly understand the method you use in order to achieve consistent results.

Never consider an exposure meter infallible but use it more as a guide which you can interpret according to the particular subject you are photographing. Even with a built-in meter remember that exposure meters are calibrated to give an average reading and a further adjustment to the indicated reading is sometimes necessary. When taking reflected-light readings of extreme contrasts it is best to measure the brightest and darkest objects and use a mid-way setting. For general outdoor scenes always point the meter slightly downwards so that the bright sky does not influence the reading.

Some meters are fitted with a translucent plastic cover which clips over the photo-electric cell for incident-light readings. With this method the meter is pointed towards the light source from the subject position and measures the light which falls on the subject, as opposed to the reflected-light system of measuring the light which is reflected from the subject back to the camera.

There is less exposure latitude with colour film than with black and white, especially with colour reversal film. Colour negative film can be considered to have more tolerance as some compensation can be made at the printing stage, when slight colour casts can also be corrected. Nevertheless, it is advisable to refer to an exposure meter if you are striving for award-winning quality. A reliable method for determining accurate exposure for colour film is to base your reading on the middle tones.

When exposing colour reversal films, even slight

'Contemporary Style': A picture which judges have been very positive about in their assessment, either admiring it enormously or not appreciating the picture at all. Photographed near a highway in the USA, it was the modern design and the colour of the tiles that was the attraction. To give emphasis to the style, the shot was under-exposed to eliminate some detail in the shadow areas.

Exhibited a number of times including a District Arts Association exhibition.

OM-1   Kodachrome 64   75-150mm zoom   1/125th sec @ f8

17

over-exposure will reduce the strength of colour. One whole stop over-exposure can easily result in the transparency displaying weak washed-out colours, with no detail in the highlights. An over-exposed transparency which might be considered just about passable if viewed 'hand-held', would never be considered acceptable by competition standards if projected on to a screen. Conversely, slight under exposure will increase the colour saturation and often render a far more pleasing result.

Although incident–light meters are preferable for colour reversal film, even with an incident reading, correction is sometimes necessary for all light scenes such as an open beach or a light coloured building, when the indicated exposure should be reduced by half a stop. A similar change in exposure should be made for dark scenes when half a stop more exposure should be allowed. For a meter which is calibrated for reflected light, the corrections are exactly in reverse: for an all light scene you increase exposure and for all dark scenes less exposure should be given.

If you are striving for colour pictures which will withstand the scrutiny of the judging panels you will find that by experimenting with exposure, you will learn the benefits of exposure variation and the techniques required to obtain saturated or soft colours. Although it can be asserted that so-called correct exposure will contribute to an accurate representation of the scene photographed, both over and under exposure can be used to create an effect. Determining exposure to give unusual results is not easy. So always make a note of your exposure variations for future reference.

Whenever you think you have an unrepeatable prize-winning scene in your viewfinder, and there is opportunity for more than one shot, it is worth bracketing the exposure, which means taking additional photographs at one-half or one stop above and below the setting indicated by the exposure meter.

'Silhouette': Backlighting is not easy to use, but the results can be outstanding. There is no such thing as correct exposure for a backlit scene, but it is important that the photograph conforms to the result you want. One way of increasing your chance of success is to bracket your exposures by shooting additional shots above and below the exposure selected. The difficulty with a picture like 'silhouette' is maintaining detail in the highly reflective sea. The even colours of the sky and mountain range have provided pleasing bands of colour.

Camera club award in a transparency competition.

OM-1   Ektachrome 64   75-150mm zoom   1/125th sec @ f5.6

Films

From the range of films available in colour and black-and-white, the variety of film speeds can be divided into three groups:

Slow Film: ISO (ASA/DIN) 25/15° to ISO 50/18°: Films in this group give very fine grain, excellent sharpness and detail.

Medium Film: ISO (ASA/DIN) 64/19° to ISO 160/23°: Good all-round film with fine grain structure and some exposure latitude.

Fast Film: ISO (ASA/DIN) 200/24° to ISO 400/27°: Fast films have a wide exposure latitude and are ideal for low light conditions.

Black-and-white film and some colour reversal film can be uprated to give a workable exposure for action or low-light photography, without a great loss of quality. Any change in the rating requires adjustment to be made in the processing, so before uprating any film ensure that your processing laboratory will accept the particular brand of film, or for home processing check the instruction sheet. Whenever a film is uprated remember that all frames should be exposed at the higher rating. Colour negative film must always be rated at the manufacturer's recommended film speed.

Although there is not a film which is suitable for every occasion, for competition photography a black-and-white film of medium speed (ISO 125/22°) is an excellent general purpose film. It is an ideal compromise between the very fine grained slow films and the group of fast films which are suitable for dull lighting and high shutter speeds but contain coarser grain. Try to extend your photographic range by using both slow and fast films, but first acquaint yourself with films in the medium speed group.

Medium speed film will cope with most subjects and lighting conditions, enabling the use of apertures and shutter speeds which will obviate camera shake. An important characteristic is its latitude, which is useful for overcoming errors in exposure or development. Nevertheless, the combination of medium speed film and correct development will produce excellent negatives suitable for considerable enlargement to exhibition standard.

From the wide choice of colour films available a film speed of ISO 100/21°, is a popular choice for colour negatives because of its sharpness and fine grain qualities.

For colour reversal film ISO 64/19° is a reasonable speed for most subjects and has good grain qualities. Among the colour reversal films available are Kodachrome 25 and 64 which have to be returned to the manufacturer for processing.

In many colour contests, entries may be submitted as prints or slides, which gives you the advantage of sending entries from the film you normally use—either colour negative film for colour prints or colour reversal film if you prefer transparencies. If you take only transparencies, remember that satisfactory colour prints can be obtained from good quality transparencies, but some of the original colour rendering may be lost in the reproduction.

Reversal films can be divided into further groups: daylight type film, and tungsten film suitable for artificial light. It is possible to use one type of colour reversal film with another light source; this is achieved by using one of the appropriate conversion filters which are available to provide the correct colour balance, but an increase in exposure is necessary. Blue flashbulbs, flashcubes and electronic flashgun units are balanced for use with daylight colour films.

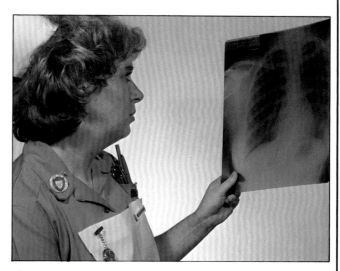

'Community Nurse': The choice of viewpoint and lighting is of paramount importance when you are photographing someone involved with their work. To avoid competing detail I chose a plain background, which also helped to show some detail in the X-ray film. Illumination was provided by photofloods.

An award winner in a camera club exhibition.

Rolleiflex T   Ektachrome 160 (Tungsten)   75mm lens 1/15th sec @ f5.6

Of the various colour films available it should not be assumed that one brand of film will render results which are superior to the others. People differ considerably in their opinion and appreciation of colour. If a group of photographers were asked to think of the colour yellow, it is likely that each one would visualize a different shade. Film manufacturers, too, produce emulsions which represent their particular interpretation of colour. Whereas some films are warmer overall, others give a more subdued, cooler result. A certain film might be excellent in bright conditions but respond poorly when the day is dull. Conversely, another emulsion might be expected to indicate more contrast when the sky is overcast.

Filters

It has been emphasized that expensive equipment is not a prerequisite for creative prize-winning photography. But there are accessories marketed which undoubtedly increase the scope of any camera system; filters come into this category and will prove to be an asset in producing imaginative pictures.

There are two shapes of filter to consider. One is the conventional circular screw-in kind and the other is a square type that slides into a holder which is attached to an interchangeable adapter. A benefit of the latter style is that if you should change your camera or buy an additional lens which takes a different filter size, you need only purchase another adapter.

A yellow filter is one of the most popular for black-and-white photography. Being a complementary colour to blue, it is particularly useful for darkening blue sky just enough to give some prominence to white clouds. It also ensures that a clear blue sky reproduces as a light grey tone and not white paper in the finished print.

When using filters, exposures should be increased by the manufacturer's recommended filter factor. Ensure that exposures are kept to a minimum, as over exposure will reduce the filter's effect. A filter factor indicates the necessary additional exposure. Therefore, a x2 factor requires the exposure to be doubled. Instead of a camera setting of 1/60th of a second at f11, a x2 factor would need 1/60th of a second at f8. A x4 factor would require two stops increase in exposure, consequently 1/60th of a second at f11 would become 1/60th of a second at f5.6.

A rule to remember is that filters will lighten objects of similar colour and darken those of complementary colour.

Opposite page: 'Natural Backdrop': The star effect was created by stopping down a wide-angle lens to its smallest aperture and including the sun in the photograph. Although the branches of the trees appear in silhouette, the leaves have retained some translucency. The repetition of size and shape of the trees provide the pattern of the picture but the appeal of the composition is dependent entirely on the star effect and the surrounding area of brightness.
Camera club competition award.
OM-1   Kodachrome 64   28mm lens   1/60th sec @ f16

Two very useful filters which do not require an increase in exposures are the UV/Haze filter, which absorbs excess ultra-violet light without affecting colour balance, and a Skylight filter which also absorbs ultra-violet light and eliminates the blue colour cast in pictures taken under a clear blue sky, or in scenes near the coast and distant landscapes.

In addition to the filters listed at the end of this chapter, there are also special effects filters and attachments which give a wide choice of variation for any specified shot and aid the photographer in accomplishing unusual and dramatic results. Among those available are cross screen, dual colour, fog, multi-image, soft focus, and star filters. One way of reproducing a star effect without a filter is to stop down a standard or wide-angled lens to its smallest aperture and to include the sun in the picture. Graduated filters are described in the section on Special Effects.

'St. Michael's Mount': It is always easy to be wise after you see the results. If I were to photograph this scene again under similar conditions I would probably use an orange filter instead of a yellow one as in this picture. My intention when composing the shot was to emphasize the mount and not make the sky too prominent. The wave nearest the beach was also darkened slightly to give the picture a good base. This sort of picture usually does well in Photographic Society and Club competitions.
   A camera club exhibition award winner.
Rolleiflex T   Ilford FP4   75mm lens (yellow filter)   1/500th sec @ f8

FILTERS FOR COLOUR PHOTOGRAPHY

Filter	Factor	Effect
Skylight	None	Absorbs excess ultra-violet light and reduces blue colour cast in photographs taken under clear blue sky. Suitable for scenes near coast and distant landscapes.
UV/Haze	None	Absorbs excess ultra-violet light as Skylight filter but does not add warmth to colour film.
Neutral Density	x2 x4	Reduces the intensity of light without affecting colour balance or contrast.
Polarizing	x3	Subdues reflections from non-metallic surfaces such as glass, polished wood, water, etc. Darkens blue sky.
Conversion A - D	x2	Allows Type A artificial light film to be used in daylight.
Conversion D - A	x4	Allows Type D daylight film to be used in artificial light.

The two conversion filters listed above are from a range of orange and blue filters used for correcting colour balance.

FILTERS FOR BLACK AND WHITE PHOTOGRAPHY

Filter	Factor	Effect
Light Yellow	x2	Darkens blue slightly. Gives emphasis to clouds by darkening blue sky.
Medium Yellow	x3	As above but more pronounced.
Yellow-Green	x2	Lightens yellow and green, darkens blue and red slightly. Suitable for landscapes and foliage.
Green	x3	Renders green lighter, darkens blue and red. Ideal for fields and trees which appear too dark.
Orange	x4	Lightens yellow and red, darkens blue, also darkens green slightly. Accentuates clouds and penetrates haze. Subdues freckles in portraits.
Red	x7	Lightens red and darkens blue and green. Gives dramatic cloud effects and penetrates distant haze.
UV/Haze	None	Absorbs excess ultra-violet (also suitable for colour film). For high altitudes, seascapes and snow scenes.
Polarizing	x3	Subdues reflections from non-metallic surfaces such as glass, polished wood, water, etc.

Never leave filters unprotected when not in use. Take care of them as you would your lens, keeping the surfaces free from dust and finger marks and cleaning them only with a soft lens brush or lens cleaning tissue.

Flash

No photographer's equipment holdall can be considered complete without a flashgun, which is a very efficient provider of instant light with a colour balance similar to daylight. Just as there are different types of cameras, so there are many kinds of flash units.

The automatic or computerized flashgun simplifies calculations by the means of a photo-electric sensor which controls the amount of light by switching off when sufficient light has been reflected from the subject back to the flashgun. There are also flash units of the dedicated type that are designed to be used with specific cameras. However, most automatic flashguns incorporate a manual setting.

Manual flashguns usually display a table which indicates aperture settings for flash to subject distance, or a calculator disc which can be set to the ISO (ASA/DIN) rating of the film to give the aperture for the distance required.

To work out camera settings for a manual flashgun you must use the guide number appropriate for the speed rating of the film. The number is divided by the distance in feet that the flashgun is from the subject, the result will give the aperture to be used with the shutter speed recommended for flash on your camera. In other words, if the flashgun guide number for the film is 100 and the subject is 9 feet away, by dividing 100 by 9 you would arrive at an aperture of f11. Always check whether the guide number is applicable to feet or metres.

The duration of flash of an electronic unit is much shorter than the superseded expendable-bulb flashguns, which are rarely seen now apart from cube assemblies, therefore the 'x' setting on the camera must be used.

A flashgun fixed on the camera accessory shoe does give acceptable results but tends to produce shots of uninspiring flat lighting. For flash pictures intended as possible competition entries, extra control over the lighting is needed. This can be effected by attaching an extension lead from the camera to the flashgun, enabling the flashgun to be held a little above the camera in order to throw the shadows downwards and to one side, to give some modelling to the subject. Until you become familiar with the various effects an extension lead can achieve, do not hold the flashgun more than a foot or so from the camera and avoid placing your subject too close to the background.

One way of eliminating heavy shadows is to employ the bounced flash technique; the illumination being provided by reflected light. The flashgun is

'Passing Interest': A District Council will sometimes arrange a competition to celebrate an anniversary of an ancient building or to highlight a certain event. As was the case when a council challenged local photographers to capture atmospheric scenes around the district. The council had been invited to participate in the Council of Europe's Water's Edge campaign, designed to publicize and help conserve areas 'where land and water meet'. After thinking of ways to interpret the theme, arrival at the chosen location indicated that with the dark clouds there would be little choice of the sun shining. Water being an excellent reflector did give some sparkle but the only alternative was to use flash in an attempt to lighten the boy's face. The effort was worthwhile because the print won first prize of a trophy and a gift voucher in the monochrome section.

Bronica SQA   Ilford FP4   80mm lens   1/60th sec @ f5.6

pointed to the ceiling at an angle of approximately 45° in the direction of the subject. The ceiling, preferably white, becomes a reflector and gives a balanced light which eliminates dense shadows. Exposure is calculated by using the guide number in the normal way and increasing the exposure by two stops. Alternatively the guide number can be divided by the flash-to-ceiling-to-subject distance and then the aperture is opened by one extra stop. The reflective value of surfaces varies considerably but accurate exposure can be consistently obtained once you have ascertained the surface you intend to use. Always take care to avoid direct light from the flash falling on the lens. Once you become familiar with the method, bounced flash will prove to be a versatile and reliable source of lighting, giving even illumination, soft shadows and good modelling.

Another form of bounced flash which is widely used by professionals is the brolly-flash system. The umbrellas are a matt silver colour or white nylon and the flashgun is fitted into an accessory shoe at the base of the brolly. The flash is directed at the middle of the canopy which gives a diffused but directional form of lighting, which is especially pleasing for portraits. If possible, the brolly should be supported on a tripod. Once you obtain satisfactory exposures which are based on your equipment and the brolly manufacturer's suggestions, you can confidently achieve controlled results for any location and devote your attention to the subject matter.

It is only when you become completely familiar with your equipment and materials that you can be entirely preoccupied with the composition of your pictures.

A Guide to Winning Themes

Photographers often have a special interest in a certain branch of photography such as sport, portraits, nature, landscape, or animal pictures. Beginners too, will soon discover the kind of photographs they enjoy taking most. If your favourite subjects are children and animals, then concentrate on competitions which include those categories.

When entering a competition, first of all explore the theme and try to ascertain the sort of photographs the judging panel is likely to be looking for. Then make a list of ideas which you consider would be relevant to the contest. For an open competition determine the kind of picture content which could be of maximum appeal to the sponsors or most fitting to the style of the periodical in which the contest appears. For instance, the judges of an open competition in a camping magazine are more likely to be impressed with photographs depicting scenic views and the outdoor life.

Favourite Subjects

The majority of photographic competitions are promoted during the summer months, therefore it is not surprising that many of them are those with a holiday theme. The contests are often advertised on a nation-wide basis, offering excellent prizes to the winners, and attracting thousands of entries.

'Happy Holidays' or 'Summer Snapshots' are the

'Up and Over': Most people take pictures while on holiday, which is why there is always a tremendous response to any competition with a holiday theme. Unfortunately the majority of pictures entered fall short of the organizers' requirements. Far too many shots display static beach scenes of people awkwardly posed. Others will show adults and children who have stopped their game to turn towards the camera. Though the surroundings may be delightful, the results will lack the spontaneity required. Although this shot was arranged, its success in holiday contests indicates the sort of picture the sponsors look for.

An award winner in an *Evening News* 'Holiday Mood' Competition, a *True* magazine Holiday Contest, and a Holiday Photo Competition in aid of a Charitable Trust.

Rolleiflex T   Ilford FP3   75mm lens   1/500th sec @ f5.6

'Fun Time:' To strive for originality is commendable, but there are occasions when a successful formula can be repeated. A number of years had elapsed since 'Up and Over' had first won a holiday picture competition, so I revived the idea to enter a contest called Kodak/Royal Mail Postcard Competition. In addition to a prize of a holiday all winners would have their photographs reproduced as a picture postcard.

'Fun Time' is one of a few shots I took for the competition. My entry did not reach the heights of a top award, but the old idea did qualify for one of the runners up prizes—a best selling book on photography.

Bronica ETRS   Ektachrome 64   75mm lens   1/250th sec @ f5.6

sort of titles frequently given to these popular contests, and indicate the picture element the sponsors seek. The average holiday contest allows plenty of freedom for imaginative photography, provided you observe the theme in your interpretation.

For success in this type of specified competition it is essential to submit pictures which contain happy, lively interest. Any shot which shows people engaged in enjoyable activity stands more chance of impressing the judges than the familiar camera-conscious pose so often found in family albums. Whenever you record a holiday incident try to capture the happiness of the occasion.

At the seaside the natural surroundings of boats, break-waters and rocks are ready-made props, which can be incorporated to add authentic dimensions to your picture arrangements. A beach game can take on additional impact if framed between the supporting beams of a jetty. A commonplace subject of children building sandcastles can come to life from a low viewpoint.

Pictures of a farm holiday can be transformed from a mediocre family record by including farming implements or machinery as a backcloth to children at play.

A photograph in which people appear uneasy and static will always lose points to the shot which displays a slice of life or action. If you are photographing people and it is necessary to pose them, the final result should never reveal this.

Pictures to Avoid

One way of overcoming the difficulty of a posed set-up is to instruct your models to turn towards the camera, or agreed position, a moment before you press the exposure release. A contrived smile can then become a relaxed expression and result in a natural-looking photograph. Avoid submitting hackneyed subjects such as swans, children eating ice-cream, or well-known beauty spots, unless you have a really outstanding shot.

Photography is a hobby which extends beyond the summer season, apart from the aid of flash or fast film, numerous subjects can be found during the winter months as well.

It must be said that in open competitions, human interest pictures will often score over subjects such as architecture or landscape. That is not to suppose a landscape of outstanding pictorial quality will not win first prize in an open competition, but with other attributes such as originality and technique being equal it is fair to say that an activity or a human aspect picture will usually succeed.

The competition which leaves the choice of subject to the contestant can sometimes cause difficulty when you are deciding on the kind of picture to submit, especially when the rules specify that an entry should comprise more than one photograph. For the photographer who specializes in one subject such as

sport or candid pictures, the theme is obvious, but for someone who enjoys a wide range of subjects, a selection of pictures depicting people and activity would be preferable to quiet pastoral scenes.

An important point in an open contest is to note any reference to the number of photographs which may be submitted. If it is stated that 'up to three prints may be entered', it suggests that the pictures will be judged individually. However, if a set of three prints is requested then you should submit photographs which maintain some conformity in style and choice of subject.

When you select a set of pictures for a contest always choose photographs which are strong in subject matter yet benefit by being presented together. For example, a set of prints could comprise three landscapes each of a different location but linked together by the type of printing paper and the apparent technique of the photographer.

Finding Inspiration

When you are considering entering a contest with no fixed theme and cannot find inspiration for ideas, start by thinking about all the subject matter waiting to be explored outside your own front door. Make a list of possible pictures and set yourself an assignment. Alternatively re-look at some of the photographs you have shot in the past, scrutinize them and note where improvements could be made in composition, choice of view-point, lighting conditions and time of day. This is always a good exercise because faults which have not been noticed before will suddenly become glaringly obvious. In a short time you will have collated a list of improvements upon which you can plan a fresh approach in an imaginitive way.

Subjects are all around you—old churches, derelict buildings, redevelopment areas and public parks. The foregoing alone should provide a number of ideas. You can always visit locations near home without taking your camera and simply assess the possibilities for photography and whether early or late sunlight would be an advantage.

The newcomer to photography may feel diffident at tackling a specific set-subject competition for the first time, but a set theme can provide the inspiration for you to take pictures of subject matter you would not normally consider. A confident knowledge of the equipment to be used and a carefully planned approach are basic steps to success. The following notes are a guide for some of the more popular categories.

Action

For action shots of a powerboat leaping across the waves or the antics of a group of clowns in a carnival procession, load your camera with a fast or medium speed film. This enables a high shutter speed to be used together with a small aperture which permits a

'Splash-down': A boat of holiday-makers hitting the water with a splash, was entered in a newspaper contest which ran for a few months. A cash prize was awarded to the photographer of each picture published. A fast shutter speed was used to freeze the action and obtain as much detail as possible.

Winner of a £5 prize in the *Evening Standard* 'Amateur Cameraman at Large' contest.

Rolleiflex T   Ilford FP3   75mm lens   1/500th sec @ f5.6

'Rushing Waters': Waterfalls, an element of nature, are familiar yet still challenging to a photographer. Usually choice of viewpoint gives opportunity to attempt alternative interpretations of the flowing water. An elevated position permitted me to look down and frame an inverted 'L' shape of the rock formation. When you are close to a waterfall it can be difficult to assess the various areas and the likely effect on the composition. One way of overcoming the difficulty is to view the continuous movement with half-closed eyes to enable you to evaluate the light and dark waters which will appear as tones in the photograph.

Camera club exhibition award.

Bronica ETRS   Ilford FP4   75mm lens   1/30th sec @ f5.6

greater depth of field. When enlargements are required from a small area of the negative a medium speed film is preferable.

When a reasonable depth of field can be utilized, the camera can be pre-focused on an area where it is anticipated the subject will be when the shutter release is pressed. This method is referred to as zone-focusing.

With action photography, the subject's speed is not the only consideration. The direction in which the subject is moving and its distance from the camera are also influencing factors. To arrest movement which passes across the line of vision a much faster shutter speed is required than would be needed to record action which moves towards or away from the camera position.

As an approximate guide, a person walking towards the camera at 30 feet would require a shutter speed of 1/60th of a second, or if approaching the camera diagonally across the field of view, 1/125th of a second. For someone walking directly across the field of view 1/250th of a second would be necessary.

When shooting action photographs of groups, resist the habit of taking every picture either from eye or waist level. Try a variation in the sequence by using a viewpoint nearer to the ground. By adopting this method you can isolate the group against the sky and so eliminate unwanted background detail which would compete visually with the action.

Movement can always be indicated by using a slow shutter speed. Interesting blurred action shots of children on roundabouts or swings can be effectively achieved in this way. Alternatively, by using a fast shutter speed, movement can be frozen at a point when, for example, the upward motion of a swing reaches its farthest extent and is momentarily suspended at the peak of action prior to its downward sweep.

There are times when freezing the action will result in a lifeless picture such as when a moving car seems to be stationary or a bird in flight photographed with a fast shutter speed appears to be motionless. Although this can also happen from time to time with flash, do not be deterred from using flash to freeze the movement of animals as well as birds. Most people will have seen some of the excellent examples of natural history pictures which have been obtained with electronic flash.

When photographing action or movement of any kind, especially for a competition, try something more than simply arresting the action with a 1/500th or 1/1000th shutter speed. One type of picture already referred to which will stand out, is a shot that displays an impression of action in the form of a blur or a distorted image. By this interpretation of movement, the kind of subject matter which is frequently submitted to photographic contests can be transformed to a standard that is strikingly different.

Waterfalls are an example of this; to the eye they appear as a cascade of sparkling movement, yet when reproduced on a sheet of printing paper the eye-catching quality of the original scene can be dull and non-effective. Exposures of 1/15th to 1/8th of a second are slow enough to give an impression of movement and can convey the effect of rushing water. By mounting the camera on a tripod, the surrounding rocks and foliage can be recorded in sharp detail

'Cascade': The picture was composed so that the arrangement would emphasize the 'S' shaped flow of the water. A slow shutter speed helped to achieve this by blurring the detail of the fast flowing current. Rocks, stones and some areas of water with comparatively slow movement have served to create the impression.
Accepted for the Rutland Water Show Photographic Exhibition.

OM-1   Kodachrome 25   28mm lens   1/15th sec @ f8

which will intensify the appearance of the swirling water.

When planning an action entry for a competition always strive to be imaginative in your interpretation of the ideas that come to mind. There are the occasions when the photographer has very little control over the amount of subject movement, but it is possible to tackle the action in alternative ways as previously described. A good routine to follow which enables you to obtain a variety of pictures is to try a few shots at the peak of the action or movement using a fast shutter speed such as 1/500th of a second, and then progressing to something different at slower

speeds, keeping the background sharp and emphasizing the blur. If colour film is used the various hues will accentuate the flowing lines of movement more than with black-and-white film. Nevertheless, provided good contrast is maintained, blur can be effective in black-and-white also.

Another approach to your assignment would be to hand hold a camera at slower speeds and follow the flowing sweeps of movement with a panning action, blurring the background as well as the subject matter in a deliberate attempt to create an abstract result yet still enabling the subject matter to be recognizable.

Panning is a method used for indicating an impression of movement of anything passing across your field of view, allowing you to record the subject in sharp focus with the rest of the area remaining blurred. (This is also referred to in the section on sport.) To maintain focus on a moving subject requires some practice until you are confident of adjusting focus correctly. The aperture setting is as important as the shutter speed, so the depth of field

'City Scene': Taking pictures of well-known landmarks and buildings and trying to present them in a different way from the usual viewpoints, is difficult but sometimes rewarding. Trying to improve your visual awareness and seeking to present a familiar scene in a new way can culminate in a picture suitable for a competition or the exhibition wall. In the photograph taken in Trafalgar Square, the viewpoint was chosen to record the screen of water in the middle distance and to give emphasis to the foreground shapes.

This picture has gained a camera club award and has been exhibited in the East of England Show Exhibition.

Rolleiflex T   Ilford FP4   75mm lens   1/250th sec @ f11

scale should be checked carefully to ensure the result required.

The most relaxed stance for panning is to stand with your feet placed at a comfortable distance apart, and then once you have aligned the subject in the viewfinder, follow the movement by swinging your body from the hips in a continuous motion ensuring that you follow through smoothly until after the shutter has closed. It is essential to keep the image exactly in the same position in the viewfinder without having to hurry or slow down.

For competition photography it should be remembered that when a photograph is blurred to the extent that the subject cannot be easily identified, it sometimes requires a caption or at least a title to explain the image. Although this is acceptable, a print should not depend on a caption to explain its presence as a competition entry, because it is only in the final assessment that a title is likely to get noticed.

Whether you choose to convey action by blur or arresting the subject movement in mid-air, remember that the success of a picture is also dependent on the positioning of the activity in the frame. A speeding car will always appear more powerful if positioned off-centre in the picture with more space in front of the vehicle that at the rear. A photograph of a pedestrian will be more balanced if the person is walking into the main area of the picture rather than being positioned near the edge and looking out of the photograph.

One should never be short of subject matter for action shots, ranging from street scenes featuring traffic and people at rush hour to the movement and tracery of car lights recorded by long exposures after dark. Street scenes by day and night are popular subjects among photographers but a varied approach can be rewarding. For example, a straightforward shot of car lights may be pleasing and display an adequate

'Rush Hour': For the idea I had in mind, and a slow shutter speed of 1/15th second, the camera would normally be supported by a tripod, but at a busy junction in the City of London, it was not possible. As a waist-level viewfinder was being used the camera strap was pulled taut when the exposure was made, to lessen the degree of camera shake. Although I obtained the impression of traffic movement that I wanted, the stationary objects would have been sharper if a tripod had been used.
    Consolation prize of colour films in an *Agfa/Camera Owner* magazine 'City Scene' competition.
Rolleiflex T   Ilford FP3   75mm lens   1/15th sec @ f16

record of movement and the after dark atmosphere, but what is required in addition to those qualities is visual evidence of the photographer's creative ability when faced with a common subject that has been seen and photographed many times before.

With action photography a number of exposures is usually necessary when you are trying to achieve a definite impression of movement or a specific amount of blur. A one-off shot which is successful is rare, so you should be prepared to expose plenty of film. Important considerations which should not be overlooked are framing the subject at the time of exposure and trimming the finished print. Both these details can affect the impression of movement which is liable to be nullified if the subject is poorly positioned in the picture area.

Animals and Birds

Animals have an immense appeal and are popular subjects for both beginners and experienced photographers. One must always be alert for the unexpected and prepared for impromptu antics which may not be repeated. It is from the ordinary sequences of natural activity that competition entries are derived.

A fast shutter speed and accurate focusing are essential when photographing kittens and puppies. For very small pets such as hamsters and caged birds, a supplementary close-up lens will be needed to fill the frame. For indoor situations, the short duration of electronic flash is a great asset for freezing movement.

Instead of mounting the flash on the camera use an extension lead to enable the flashgun to be held at an angle of 45°. This will avoid a flattening effect and render the texture of the animals more favourably. Head-on flash can also cause an unnatural appearance due to light illuminating the retinas of the animals' eyes.

One advantage of taking photographs of pets indoors is that they can be confined to one room and are less likely to roam far from the camera. It is sometimes necessary to tempt a cat or dog to a certain place by warming cushions or placing a hot water bottle beneath a blanket.

The ideal place for animal photography is outdoors. In daylight you benefit from higher shutter speeds and you can employ the zone-focusing technique. Sunlight will emphasize texture of feathers and fur, but remember, long periods of direct sunshine can cause discomfort to very young kittens and puppies.

A competition entry should be more than just a good likeness of a family pet, so the assistance of someone to cajole and encourage the animals will enable you to concentrate on picture arrangement. A knowledgeable assistant can play an important part in an animal photographic session, so it is wise to discuss ideas and strategy well beforehand and definitely not in the middle of a sequence of pictures, otherwise the pets will get bored and lose interest no matter what inducements are offered.

Apart from a sharp snap of the fingers and making animal-like noises, there are a number of ways your assistant can coax the pets into favourable poses. A well-known trick of putting a dab of butter or honey on a dog's nose will immediately provide an appealing picture of a dog licking the tit-bit. Fish paste can be used with cats and kittens in a similar way, but more often than not a piece of string or ball of wool will entice a kitten into a pleasing position. Plain backgrounds will define the animals more clearly and dark coloured pets will show up best against light

'Absent Friend': National newspapers sometimes run a photography competition on their Letters page, with a prize for the picture of the week. The dog photograph was a second attempt for the picture prize after my previous entry had been rejected. If a competition is still running it is always worth submitting another try. Although I did not have a specific competition in mind when I took the picture, contests of this kind do favour animal shots. The illumination was daylight through a large window and the slow shutter speed helped to show some movement of the dog's wagging tail. As occasionally happens, when the print was published the title was changed by the Letters page editor to 'In the dog house'.
Winner of *The Observer*'s Letters Page, £25 picture prize.
Bronica ETRS Ilford FP4   1/30th sec @ f5.6

'Paddock': While driving through Suffolk I was attracted by a backlit scene which I hoped could be presented in a creative manner. This was the first of two shots in which I tried to depict the horse and foal in their environment, the fence and shed were particularly included to achieve the effect. After a short time the animals moved into the open field and I took another shot, but the processed film confirmed it was the first exposure that had atmosphere and appeal.

Exhibited at the Essex International Salon of Photography.

Rolleiflex T   Ilford FP4   75mm lens   1/60th sec @ f5.6

areas. Try to shoot from a low viewpoint and, when working close, focus on the eyes.

Farm animals obviously require different tactics, primarily because there is not the opportunity to manoeuvre them into position as with domestic pets. A farm picture can be infused with the atmosphere of the countryside by including the surroundings and farm buildings. Unless you are photographing heads only, do not take pictures of cows or horses from a head-on position as the results will appear distorted. Many breeds of animals mingle together on a farm and such an environment can result in humour and appealing prize-winning pictures.

As in all types of photography, good lighting is very important when taking shots in a farmyard and it can be worthwhile to return at a different time of day should the light be unsuitable. Farm activity usually keeps to a routine, so if you are staying on or near a farm, it should be comparatively easy to be around for feeding and milking times. Obviously it is courteous to seek the farmer's permission first.

Zoos provide an abundance of opportunities; with so many animals to choose from you can always re-visit an enclosure if the occupants are not in a photogenic position. Once again feeding time can provide a variety of good shots, but do remember that drowsy animals do not make the best subjects, so it is vital to take your pictures before or while they are feeding, because afterwards they are less alert. Zoo feeding times start about mid-day and the times are usually displayed or printed in the zoo guide.

Animals kept in larger compounds can be a disappointment to the photographer with only a standard lens. A telephoto lens is most useful in recording a reasonably sized image on film. It is always profitable to watch an animal's movements noting the path it takes and the direction to which it turns most. Assessing mannerisms in this way can help you to pre-focus on certain areas. Try to avoid including cage bars if you can. Wire-netting can be eliminated from a picture by using a wide aperture and holding the camera with the lens near the wire, but not too close. In all circumstances it is wise to keep behind the barriers that are erected between the public and the cages. In areas where spectators cannot be eliminated from the picture, use the technique of differential focusing and select a large aperture to keep them out of focus and the background unsharp.

Zoo animals can appear out of place with a brick wall background whereas a wildlife safari park can provide scenery which is far more appropriate. A long telephoto lens is very useful for the animals that wander from the car tracks. Not all the animals will be too far away for a standard lens and some will perform and play in the vicinity of the cars. Monkeys especially, are likely to put on a display around or on a vehicle, which can result in some delightful shots. The cardinal rule is to be ready with your camera set and your finger lightly resting on the shutter release. Be prepared to expose plenty of film, on one subject if necessary, whenever you think you have a prize-winning picture in the making.

Ensure that the car windows are clean before entering the park as safety regulations will necessitate all car windows to be closed once you are inside. A rubber lens hood is especially useful when keeping your camera close to the glass in order to avoid reflections. It is also helpful if someone else does the driving so that you can concentrate entirely on taking photographs.

Bird photography is difficult yet extremely rewarding when a satisfactory picture is obtained. The enthusiast will have a good knowledge of the habits of the various species and will be aware of their characteristics and temperaments. One of the best aids to a wild-life photographer is a portable hide. It is usually a construction of water resistant canvas material which is supported by poles, secured by guy lines and has observation panels in the sides. Consideration for the birds' well-being must be maintained at all times. Any indication of distress shown by the birds should prompt an immediate withdrawal by the photographer. Although bird activity in the confines of a nest is easier to photograph, no picture is worth causing the birds to

'What a Mouth': Zoos and wildlife parks provide good opportunities for appealing animal pictures, but you sometimes have to return more than once to a particular enclosure to get the picture you want. The shot of the hippopotamus was taken on a visit to the zoo. The animals had not shown much life or interest when I first visited the enclosure. On a further visit I found the situation much the same except for one hippo in the water near the enclosure railings who suddenly responded to my camera with an open mouth.
Awarded first prize of colour film in a District Council's Exhibition of Photography.

Rolleiflex T   Ilford FP4   75mm lens   1/250th sec @ f5.6

abandon their nests. Wild-life photography should not be attempted without some guidance and a basic understanding of a fascinating pursuit.

For the uninitiated, experience can be acquired in one's local environment. It is surprising how many species can be enticed by food placed on a bird-table in the garden. Another approach is to suspend a bag of nuts from the branch of a tree.

The advantage of this is that the nuts can be positioned with regard to the background and the most convenient place for camera and tripod. A telephoto lens will enable you to maintain a distance that will not frighten the birds.

Sea birds are an excellent source of interest and picture possibilities. The common gull is a familiar

sight on the coast and provides very good subject matter and a challenge too. Capable of great speeds and manoeuvrability the gulls can display an unrivalled grace in flight as they glide effortlessly over beaches and rocks.

They are tame creatures and are always prepared to swoop down for a piece of bread held in an outstretched hand or thrown into the air. Once again the help of an assistant can be invaluable in arranging the 'bait' within the predetermined area of focus. Any focal length lens is suitable; it is really a matter of selecting an aperture to give a reasonable depth of field. Whenever possible a background of sky or cliffs is preferable to buildings situated along a promenade.

In all aspects of animal and bird photography, perseverance will be rewarded.

Architecture

Architectural photography for competitions does not have to be confined to well-known buildings and castles but should include cottages, office blocks and rows of houses where line and angles or shapes and patterns can be conveyed in a way that is more than a technical record.

Photographs of buildings will have more impact if the lighting is at an angle to the structure. Side

'Freedom': Although there were a number of seagulls in the vicinity I managed to frame one which was separated from the others. Out of a number of shots I took at the time, this was the picture which gave the best impression of space and the freedom enjoyed by a bird in flight. The blue expanse is in sharp contrast to the bird's light colour but contributes to good effect. Crop some of the sky and the picture loses impact.
·A camera club first award in a Natural History competition.

OM-1   Kodachrome 64   50mm lens   1/125th sec @ f5.6

lighting will contribute immeasurably in creating pictures of striking appearance, as well as emphasizing the detail and texture of brickwork and masonry. Shape and depth which are so often flattened with frontal lighting will be accentuated if you can avoid taking photographs with the sun shining from behind the camera. Sometimes it is more favourable to return to a location at a different time of day when the sun is illuminating a building from a better angle and giving emphasis to the feature you wish to reveal.

Old buildings and monuments provide picturesque subjects to the photographer who is willing to consider the best ways of exploiting distinguishing styles and features of specific periods of history. It is not necessary to reproduce every castle battlement in

'Steps': This picture has been highly commended by judges in photographic club and society competitions for its style and modern approach, yet this type of architectural subject would be unlikely to succeed in an open contest where it would compete with general subjects. Its strength is in arrangement and graphic approach with the print's tonal range enclosed in a heavy frame directing the viewer to the horizontal lines of the steps—the focal point of the composition.

This picture was awarded a trophy for pictorial architecture in a camera club exhibition.

Kowa 66   Ilford FP4   85mm lens   1/125th sec @ f5.6

clearest detail, but as an alternative, one can inject a suggestion of mystery or convey the atmosphere of an ancient place. This can be achieved by an unusual choice of filter, differential focusing or by utilizing a wide angle lens and choosing a viewpoint which creates an illusion of space.

When a picture of clarity and detail is required a tripod must be used, especially when taking photographs of interiors and a slow shutter speed is selected to overcome the problem of inadequate illumination. Permission is sometimes required for using a camera in certain buildings. Also if you intend to erect a tripod it is a courtesy to enquire whether it is allowed.

Although flash is suitable for interiors it is not so satisfactory for large areas. Flash can be very useful in combating excessive contrast such as when the sun shines through windows and you wish to illuminate adjacent details. Depending on the viewpoint and area to be covered, fill-in flash is ideal for lighting the shadows.

For churches with stained glass windows careful assessment of the light with an exposure meter is essential. The well-tried idea of recording rays of sunlight streaming through a window of an old building or church always heightens the appeal and mood of a picture.

Church interiors offer many opportunities to the competitive photographer. Archways, carved figures, lecterns, pew ends and pulpits usually reveal intricate

'Trinity House': Lighting is a very important factor of any photograph. When a building is brightly lit there is normally opportunity to produce a picture of strong design. In this shot the stonework benefits not only from the sunlight but also the shadows which define lines and shapes to make maximum use of the situation, the part of the building in complete shadow was eliminated from the frame.
  Essex International Salon of Photography and East of England Show Exhibition.

Rolleiflex T   Ilford FP4   75mm lens   1/250th sec @ f11

'Design': One way of finding pictures for competitions or exhibitions is to set yourself an assignment. It could be a series of pictures including a number of subjects, or you could plan to concentrate on one theme. This is a good exercise for beginners as well as the experienced photographer. That is how 'Design' came about. I set myself a plan to photograph contemporary architecture, seeking to record modern lines and shapes from various angles.
  Exhibited at the Essex International Salon of Photography.

Rolleiflex T   Ilford FP4   75mm lens   1/125th sec @ f11

craftsmanship of past generations and are ideal for photographs of detail and texture. Modern churches too, contain outstanding styles of line and pattern but without the involved detail of earlier years. Contemporary structure can be presented with boldness, employing the clear-cut designs to make pictures of contrast and shape.

Correct viewpoint is vital, a few yards' variation in the camera position can be the difference between an austere record and a creative composition. Always study a building from as many angles as possible before deciding on the most pleasing arrangement. The preliminary viewing will enable you to visualize the finished result and assess the features you wish to convey. By judicious selection in the viewfinder the

dominant aspect of a building can be maintained. In a similar way the careful inclusion of a certain shape or shadow can enhance the grandeur of the design.

A photograph for a competition does not depend upon the exact representation of an architectural subject but rather the impression the photographer has been able to convey. A picture of a building can be superb technically, displaying excellent detail and a correct perspective which shows the photographer's appreciation and feeling for the architecture. However, a picture presented in that manner reflects the skill of the architect as well as the one who made the picture, and therefore would be more appropriate to compete in a category for architectural record instead of an open contest.

'Brickwork and Stone': If this building had been photographed from a straight-on viewpoint on a dull day, the result would have been flat and uninteresting. But in this picture, the directional sunlight has revealed texture and detail, with design and shape displayed in bold relief.
   Camera club competition award.

Olympus FTL   Ektachrome 64   50mm lens   1/125th sec @ f5.6

'Lectern': A fairly bright day made it possible to produce this church interior feature by natural light. As a competition entry the reproduction of the lectern has been commended, although the picture's success rate would be higher if the windows were not so conspicuous. One of the problems when taking church interiors is that windows which occupy a small area are never as prominent in the viewfinder as they are in the processed transparency. With a print the additional brightness can be modified when enlarging.
   Camera club competition award.

OM-1   Ektachrome 64   50mm lens   1/15th sec @ f5.6

One of the problems of photographing high buildings is known as converging verticals. The trouble is caused when the camera is tilted in order to fill the viewfinder with the whole building. This difficulty can be overcome by moving farther from the building and including more foreground, provided the foreground interest will blend with or be subordinate to the main subject. Examples of foreground interest which could be utilized in this way are a driveway which leads to a stately home; a statue or waterfall situated in the grounds of a public building or the inclusion of a lich-gate when photographing a church. The golden rule is to keep the back of the camera upright. If the foreground is uninteresting, only the part of the negative containing the actual architechture need be enlarged.

When your camera is loaded with black-and-white film a yellow filter will improve the rendering of a blue sky, but for a really dramatic picture of a light coloured building against a blue sky, an orange filter should be used. A wide-angle lens will record not only a wider angle of view than a standard lens, but it will also give a greater depth of field, and is well suited to architectural work. If you find it impossible to

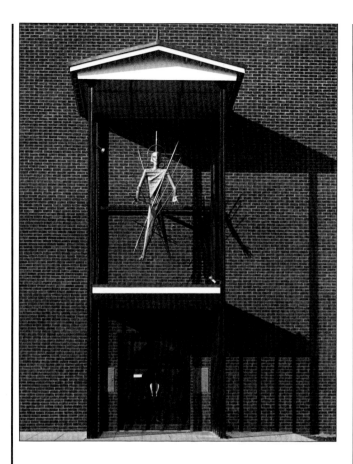

'St. Martin's': For anyone hoping to photograph a building or church under the best possible conditions it is advisable to view the structure at various times during the day to assess the most effective lighting and camera viewpoint. After trying different camera angles and moving in close to feature the canopy and figure of Christ above the porch, I decided to photograph the entrance from a straight-on viewpoint. By positioning the main feature off-centre and including the strong shadows to provide impact, the photograph gained further interest.

Camera club exhibition trophy winner.

Rolleiflex T Ilford FP4 75mm lens 1/250th sec @ f11

'Lamps': Camera clubs often find a place in their syllabus of competitions, for 'set subjects'. This is the kind of picture which would be suitable for an architectural record or feature competition. Judges have commented favourably on the shape of the lamps being repeated in shadow, and also on the rich black tones of the principal image. On the debit side criticism has been made about the distracting vertical lines of the stonework on each side of the lamps. Such comments—good and bad—spotlight one of the benefits of camera club membership where constructive criticism of your work helps to improve your skill.

The picture gained a runner-up prize in a contest organized by the *Jewish Chronicle* and an award in a camera club exhibition.

Rolleiflex T Ilford FP4 75mm lens 1/250th sec @ f8

maintain the verticals upright, produce something quite different by exaggerating the distortion instead.

In addition to considering architectural style, thought should be given to the symmetrical details and the format in which the finished picture will be presented. For example, if a high building is the prominent feature of a composition, to reproduce it in a horizontal format would nullify any idea of attracting attention to the structure's height. But as in many aspects of photography this is a basic guide which ultimately depends on individual interpretation.

Archways often comprise outstanding features and superb architectural style, and therefore make strong subjects in themselves, but always be alert to utilizing

'Mosaic Detail': The range of success for this type of photograph is very limited, but it is included as an example of pictures which can be entered in a set subject of architectural detail or feature at a local Photographic Society or Camera Club. Some exhibitions also include architectural record sections in which similar pictures to this one could be entered. Unfortunately such pictures in an open competition would stand little chance of receiving recognition.

Camera club competition award.

Olympus FTL   Ektachrome 64   50mm lens   1/125th sec @ f5.6

'Mosque El Aksa': Taken in Jerusalem, the scene is bathed by the late afternoon sunshine which accentuates the silver dome and the architecture. Different judges have commented on the striking effect of the arches and the stonework of the supports which contrast with the darker area. The photograph also benefits from a cloudless sky reproduced as an even tone which is complementary to the architecture.

Camera club exhibition award winner.

Rolleiflex T   Ilford FP4   75mm lens   1/125th sec @ f8

'On the Temple Mount': Whenever you have the opportunity to photograph a well-known place, there is no reason why you should not take a picture from the traditional viewpoint. For the competition photographer however, the next step is to find an alternative camera position that will not only enhance the subject but give a result that will be good enough to stand out from other competition entries. It is not uncommon in photo-contests for similar pictures of well-visited locations to be submitted. In this shot the angle of view, archway detail and lighting were enough to influence the judge to award the transparency first place in a camera club open subject competition.

OM-1   Ektachrome 64   50mm lens   1/125th sec @ f5.6

an archway as a frame to another structure. When using an archway or opening for this purpose, it is not always the front-on view which is the best arrangement. By shooting the archway from an angle a dramatic interpretation can be achieved.

A competition which includes a category for architectural record pictures gives an opportunity to submit photographs of a particular detail of a building, such as an ornate window or a carved door. Record pictures can still be presented in a pictorial style, when the photographer's treatment of the subject can be of greater appeal than the subject itself.

Candid Snapshots

Instinctive reaction to an incident or an expression is the key to the kind of candid photography which is likely to achieve success in competitions. A basic objective is to remain unobserved when shooting, for while people are unaware that they are being photographed they will behave naturally and without any inhibitions. The whole purpose is to obtain unposed, interesting pictures, which represent a slice of life.

Generally, people do not like being stared at, so it is important to mingle with the crowd or to keep on the move instead of remaining in an open position which will attract attention. Only a glance is necessary for someone to realize that a camera is being pointed at them. When this happens and you are discovered, continue taking pictures. The result may reveal a prize-winning candid shot indicating surprise, an ostentatious pose or even an attitude of indignation. When people do show annoyance it it best to move on. Alternatively a smile in the direction of your subject will infer that there is nothing untoward in your intentions. Usually people enjoy the attention and respond by posing but this is the last thing a candid photographer wants.

When setting out to take candid photographs ensure that your camera is ready for instant use, even to the point of having the ever-ready case unfastened. Set the shutter to 1/250th of a second and the focus to somewhere between twelve and twenty feet. Always check that the aperture is set according to the exposure meter reading.

A photograph can be lost in the time it takes you to glance at your camera to confirm that the settings are right. Always take the shot first, then refer to the controls to check that exposure and distance are correct. Get into the habit of taking exposure readings at regular intervals especially when you are searching for candid pictures in areas of sunlight and shadow or planning an effect you want for a shot against the light. Try to memorize the shutter speed and aperture required in relation to the direction you will be pointing the camera.

When you find a suitable subject, simply position yourself at the distance pre-set on the camera, this will dispense with the operation of focusing each time; furthermore, you will attract the minimum of attention and so improve your chances of shooting some outstanding candid pictures. A camera held to the eye can be conspicuous so whenever possible conceal your camera the best you can and bring the camera to your eye only when you are ready to press the shutter release. With this approach a standard lens

'Glimpse of the past': The period costume, the building and the shadowed face were the features which came together for a candid shot. If the young lady had turned to the camera the spontaneity would have been lost. So it was a matter of pre-setting the camera, moving to the estimated distance and quickly taking the shot.
A camera club competition award.

OM-1 Kodachrome 64   75-150mm zoom   1/125th sec @ f8

will be quite adequate for a diverse range of subjects.

Some people feel self-conscious when they shoot candids for the first time, but after a while the sense of inhibition is usually lost in the interest of searching for subject matter. The use of a wide-angle lens will give a greater impression of involvement in the final result as well as a depth of field ranging from a few feet to infinity. A wide-angle lens means a much closer approach so the chances of being seen are increased. However, provided you are dexterous as well as familiar with your camera, you can raise the camera to your eye, fire the shutter and wind on the film as you

'Punch and Judy Fans': As the show proceeded the youngsters became more and more captivated by the drama. I first attempted to get some shots of a little lad near the front excitedly gesticulating as the plot unfolded. However, the children were too close to each other so I decided on a group shot, parents and all. The children were so absorbed that not one of them looked towards the camera.

A camera club award winner.

Ilford Sportsman 35mm
Camera Ektachrome 45mm lens 1/50 sec @ f8.

lower the camera in a succession of quick movements. Another method of obtaining candid pictures without the person's knowledge is to keep the camera away from your eye and to press the shutter release with the camera resting on your chest, with this idea it is worth experimenting with a 'practice' film first.

A telephoto lens can also provide results which give a feeling of involvement in the picture. The longer lens gives you the advantage of shooting from a greater distance, and provides an out-of-focus background, but requires precise focusing. The procedure you follow will depend on your equipment, technique and whatever way you feel most at ease. Once you are relaxed you will increase the likelihood of obtaining satisfactory results.

A twin-lens reflex camera is also suitable for candid pictures, especially as it can be fired from the waist, with the lens pointed to the left or right. If someone does become suspicious of your camera and you want to imply that you are not photographing them, the ploy of looking in another direction while pressing the shutter release, is usually successful. People assume that a picture is being taken only when the photographer is peering through the viewfinder.

Pageants, fetes and similar events are full of subjects for the candid photographer and will provide plenty of scope for this type of informal photography. People playing and enjoying leisure activities appear to lose their inhibitions. When they relax on outdoor occasions people tend to ignore a camera, and so the expressions and antics of participants and onlookers can be captured far more easily.

Markets are intriguing hunting grounds for pictures of people, their gestures and the colourful happenings of trading activity. It has already been recommended to press the shutter release before an opportunity passes, you can then make any necessary adjustments and take a second picture. You can also decide whether to move closer or to include more of the adjacent area. However, quite often it is the first exposure which conveys the spontaneous element. One cannot afford to be too selective about backgrounds; it is advisable to accept a scene just as it is, rather than miss a photograph while searching for a better background. With this type of photography, composition and ideal lighting conditions are of secondary importance to recording natural, unposed pictures.

In recent years wedding photography has evolved from the well established traditional poses but there is still a wealth of candid pictures for the alert photographer.

Whenever you are invited as a guest, take your camera and be ready for the unguarded moment. Ensure that you do not impede the official photographer in any way. It is also a courtesy to inform the photographer beforehand of your intentions so that no misunderstanding can arise.

When engaged in candid photography always maintain a sense of good judgement. Never take a picture which could cause embarrassment to others or infringe another person's privacy. If you are confronted with a situation which in your mind is questionable, be discreet and do not take the picture.

Children

The appeal of children is universal; they are natural performers who can be encouraged into photogenic positions. Young children especially, are bundles of energy, bouncing, jumping, running and always ready for a game. In outdoor surroundings, trees and garden gates are ready-made props for delightful child studies. Bushes and fences can also strengthen a composition as out-of-focus background.

'Little Joker': So often an otherwise good portrait can be spoiled by the subject's hands. If they are to be included in a prominent way, care should be taken so that they appear naturally placed. The boy's hands in the picture are close enough to the face to be a strong part of the composition. The distortion caused by the glass, complement the mischievous pose which was taken by natural window light.
Runner-up prize in *She* magazine's Photographer of the Year competition.

OM-1   Kodachrome 64   50mm lens   1/15th sec @ f5.6

When a group of youngsters are involved in a game, the sight of a camera may divert their interest momentarily but provided the photographer maintains a casual manner, they will soon return to their play again. With lively children, the direction of action is unpredictable. If the game covers a large area it is worth focusing on a pre-selected point and waiting until the fun reaches the place in focus.

Older children can be encouraged to co-operate, especially in pre-planned pictures, perhaps in a game of conkers or splashing about in a swimming pool. After a briefing and a rehearsal they will quickly become engaged in the activity, and will often introduce their own improvisations.

Unless you are producing a formal portrait, never pose a child, but do give careful consideration to backgrounds, particularly indoors where furniture, ornaments and wallpaper patterns can be too dominant. Depth of field can be reduced by using a large aperture which will put the background out of focus.

Spontaneous expressions and movement should be the aim in child photography. This can be achieved by arranging the situation beforehand. When photographing a small child an example of this would be to sit the youngster in a high chair with playbricks or a suitable toy. Once the child is engrossed, it is a matter of waiting for the right moment. The use of a tripod is invaluable for positioning and setting up the camera

'Early one morning': When submitting pictures of children to a competition ensure that the shots depict some form of activity or show an impromptu expression. Such details are essential, especially in a pre-planned picture when the results should display spontaneity. The picture of two children stepping out of a tent was not arranged in elaborate detail, but an attempt was made to keep the action as natural as possible.

Awarded a cash prize in a weekly competition sponsored by the *Church of England* newspaper.

Bessa 1   Ilford FP3   1/100th sec @ f8

'Happiness': When photographing children there are times when you can arrange a situation in advance then let the fun take its course. The strong side lighting clearly separated the boy from the background of foliage and shadow. The dark background also depicted the water spray effectively. The camera was mounted on a tripod so that the viewpoint remained constant and a 150mm lens was used to keep the camera at a reasonable distance from the water. The hose provided a valuable lead-in, directing the eye to the excited youngster and on to the shower of water.

Camera club exhibition award.

Kowa 66   Ilford FP4   150mm lens   1/250th sec @ f8

in advance. A shutter cable release is also essential for eliminating camera shake.

The inclusion of a pet in a child picture brings together two of the most popular subjects, which consequently doubles the picture interest from a competition point of view. With very small children a natural perspective can be maintained by working from their level.

Meal times can always provide picture material of young children, but every fleeting opportunity must be grasped, so be alert for the unexpected. Birthday parties too, have a wealth of ready-made pictures for the competition minded. From the blowing-out of candles on the birthday cake to the tense concentration and excitement of musical chairs or perhaps shots of the little ones consuming jelly and cakes. A picture of a baby with his first birthday cake gained a

top award in a national competition. Although the idea was not original the picture which impressed the judging panel contained the important ingredient of happiness.

Wherever babies and young children are there will always be photographic opportunities, so it is worth working out a plan for obtaining the pictures you hope to achieve. Be prepared with extra items of equipment which may be required. For babies holding on to the edge of a cot or pram, or perhaps crawling on the floor with no interest in you or the camera, remember the sound of a rattle is usually successful in getting baby to look your way. In child photography always endeavour to focus on the eyes. No matter how appealing the facial expressions may be, if the eyes are sharp as well, the vital content of life will be added to the picture.

Toddlers too, can give you many ideas, and by following them around numerous poses will occur. Even a change of mood from laughter to tears can provide a competition shot. The day when a child progresses from a high chair to a place at the meal table is not only another phase in growing up but a time of delightful expressions and gestures. Bath-time provides many charming pictures and opportunity for bounced flash. Light is reflected from inside the bath and will help to fill in shadows, the effect of this together with the glistening water will give extra life to the pictures. A word of warning: when using colour film do not bounce your flash off a coloured wall otherwise the result will show a colour cast.

Bedtime is another important happening which can give delightful studies of outstanding appeal, with the child preparing for bed, listening to a goodnight story or simply asleep accompanied by a favourite doll.

The foregoing ideas are not new and have been photographed before, but by using the suggestions as a basis to work from they can lead to a fresh slant which can be a starting point for a competition winner.

Young children dislike being kept in one position even for a short period, so it is wise to let them continue with whatever they are engrossed in, or provide them with an alternative interest which will capture their attention. A good ploy is to have some favourite toys for the child to play with at the beginning of a session. This will put the child at ease and at the same time provide opportunity for some natural pictures.

Be prepared to shoot plenty of film and ready to capture the continually changing expressions and moods of the child. Do not bother about trying to get very young children to maintain a certain pose but keep them involved with toys or books. Once the children are absorbed, make the most of every moment.

Although it is useful to have some assistance when taking shots of children, it is advisable to have the help of one person only. So often a group of well-meaning relatives and friends all encouraging the child to smile, or constantly rearranging the youngster's clothing, can so easily upset the child and your plans.

When aiming to impress a competition judge, consider the daily routine of a child's world and decide on the type of picture you could portray best. An advantage of photographing a child in a chair or a cot is that the youngster is confined in one place for a reasonable period, enabling you to concentrate entirely on expressions and posture. Although a picture of a new born baby asleep in a cot will have immense appeal to the parents and family, it would have to be extremely good to win a competition. Instead of submitting a shot of a young baby alone, increase the appeal of your entry by sending a picture which includes the mother in the arrangement as well.

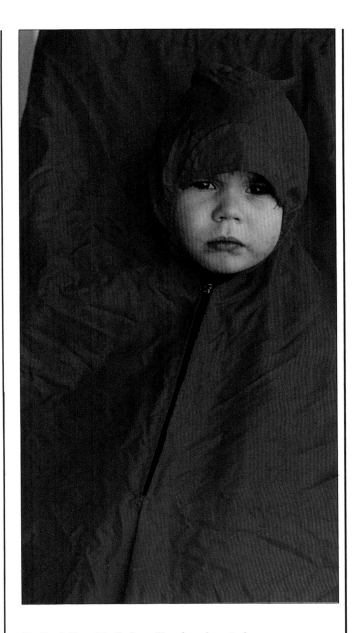

'Outlook Unsettled': A smiling face is not always a requirement for a prize-winning picture. The youngster's serious expression and the rainwear are separate elements brought together in the title. The zip-fastener was positioned diagonally as a lead-in to the child's face. It is also of value in breaking-up the large red area in the lower half of the picture.

The photograph has received a commended award for colour portraiture in the Essex International Salon of Photography and a trophy for the best colour transparency for pictorial portraiture in a camera club exhibition.

OM-1 Ektachrome 64 50mm lens 1/30th sec @ f5.6.

43

'Dreamland': A child sleeping peacefully in a cot is always worth recording on film. Although I was pleased with the result, to increase the appeal as a competition entry, some fluffy clouds were combined with the basic arrangement and achieved the desired effect and subsequent success. The picture was made by using two negatives at the enlarging stage. First, the paper was exposed to the negative of the child, during the exposure the area surrounding the image was shaded, carefully allowing some overlap of detail. Then the negative of the clouds was enlarged, while care was taken to shade the middle portion of the paper, which had been previously exposed.

The picture won a prize of colour films for being placed second in an exhibition organized to coincide with carnival week activities.

Negative of child:
Bessa 1   Ilford FP3   1/25th sec @ f16

'Puppy Love': The details of a photographic competition printed on the label of a tin of dog food specified that the judges would be selecting entries which in their opinion showed the happiest and healthiest looking dogs. It also stated that the print should be of a dog alone or with the family, which gave competitors opportunity to combine two appealing subjects—dogs and children—effectively increasing the chance of their photograph being noticed.

'Puppy Love' was submitted and won a transistor radio in the Chappie Photo Competition.

Rolleiflex T   Ilford FP4   75mm lens   1/250th sec @ f8

For very young babies, soft light is always appropriate. Available light too, is ideal for a presentation of natural appearance. Pleasing variations can be achieved by utilizing light from a window with a sheet of white card as a reflector. When including a window in your picture, net curtains will help to soften the contrast.

Close-ups

One of the most fascinating forms of photography is taking close-up pictures. With many cameras the lens focuses no closer than about three feet. Because of this some photographers ignore the possibilities of close-up shots and consequently never get near

'Winter Rose': A subject which was approached close enough to show detail on part of a rustic arch and to focus on a rose with a story of happier days. Although the ice-covered bloom displays little resemblance of its past glory, it was the veiled colour of the petals that attracted my eye and made the rose the principal interest.
  Camera club award winner.

OM-1 Ektachrome 64 50mm lens 1/60th sec @ f5.6

enough to a subject to fill the frame for maximum effect. The delicate thread of a spider's web glistening with morning dew becomes a display of silvery beauty when photographed from a few inches. A close-up of a single bloom will have much more impact as a competition entry than a view of the whole plant.

A single lens reflex camera is ideal for taking close-ups but even with a 50mm lens, the nearest you can focus down to is about twenty inches, which is insufficient for a shot of a caterpillar or for extremely small detail being photographed for unusual effect.

To get closer to the subject matter it is necessary to increase the distance between the film plane and the lens. This is achieved by inserting close-up accessories between the lens and camera body. An alternative method is to attach a supplementary lens to the front of the camera lens. Although the film to lens distance remains the same, the supplementary lens has the effect of shortening the focal length of the camera lens. Supplementary lenses do not require an increase

45

'Chestnut': When you are photographing a subject which is a small feature of an overall scene, it is essential not to be influenced by the surroundings. For this shot I framed the main interest as tightly as possible to ensure it was separated from distracting detail.
Selected for Wildlife in Trust Exhibition.
Rolleiflex T   Ektachrome   75mm lens   1/30th sec @ f16

in exposure and are available in a range of sizes to give different amounts of magnification and can be obtained individually or in sets.

One disadvantage of these special lenses is the loss of definition at the edges of a picture so it is important to use the smallest aperture possible. The nearer you are to the subject the shallower the depth of field, but with a single lens reflex camera you can see exactly how much of the subject is sharp.

For the non-reflex camera user it will be necessary to refer to the focusing calculations which are supplied with a supplementary lens. You will also require a tape measure to ensure accuracy in the positioning of your lens in relation to the subject. Also with non-reflex cameras the matter of parallax is a problem to contend with, so it is worth experimenting first and then refer to the results as a guide to overcome the danger of cutting off subject matter.

Extension tubes are easy to use and a convenient way of converting reflex cameras for close-up work. They are obtainable in sets of various sizes and are placed between the lens and camera body. The tubes can be used individually or in any combination depending on the distance to be covered.

Bellows function in a similar way to extension tubes with the advantage that they can be used in a continuous range of distances and are not restricted to the set sizes of the tubes.

Reversing rings also work on the principle of utilising your existing camera lens. A reversing ring comprises two threads, one to fit the camera lens mount and the other which screws into the filter thread on the front of the lens. The reversing ring is then mounted on to the camera body with the front of the lens facing the film. Whichever of the foregoing systems is used it is important to remember that when

the film-to-lens distance is extended, additional exposure must also be given.

Apart from accessories to convert your lens, the macro lens has become very popular in close-up photography and is designed to focus much closer than a normal lens. It gives results of exceptional sharpness and is available in a range of focal lengths.

Close-up photography is synonymous with natural history, which is a competition theme that always attracts a large entry of fascinating pictures of birds, butterflies and plants. Flowers are very suitable for close-up treatment and can be presented in numerous ways from spectacular individual blooms to the delicate translucency of petals captured in against-the-light shots. When you get close to isolate detail of small scale subjects, do not forget the depth of field limitations.

When shooting flowers in close-up it is vital to give careful thought to the background. Mostly it will appear out of focus so be wary of clustering flowers which can compete for attention. When existing surroundings are inappropriate an artificial background of coloured card is an excellent substitute. The advantage of introducing your own background is that you can experiment and make colour changes according to the separation of colour required and the blooms being photographed.

A tripod, cable release, and some string to secure flower stems in a breeze, are essential equipment as the slightest suggestion of camera shake will ruin any close-up detail.

Sometimes it is possible to isolate a bloom or a leaf against a blue sky, a polarizing filter is ideal for darkening a blue sky provided you allow an increase in exposure.

Pictures of impact which win points in competitions are often shots taken with a telephoto lens and which fill the frame wth the appearance of a close-up. With this sort of picture, filling the frame is of paramount importance and the variable focal length of a zoom lens is ideal for the exact framing of the subject.

One of the skills of picture making is to be selective; this applies to all branches of photography. Fill the viewfinder by featuring part of a scene and by deliberate arrangement make the chosen part the whole.

Extra interest will always be revealed as you move closer to a subject. If you are photographing a violinist try an alternative shot of the instrument only, isolating it from the surroundings. In a similar way you could emphasize a guitarist's hands and guitar, making a portion of the subject the finished picture. There is always a tendency, especially among beginners, to include too much subject matter without a central point, but if the picture area is filled with a close-up of a selected part, the viewer is left in no doubt of the photographer's intention. Machinery too, can be approached in the same way; by including human

'Poppy': Instead of photographing a cluster of poppies I focused on a single bloom from about eighteen inches with a standard lens. By recording the poppy in its natural setting the out-of-focus background is very important to the overall effect. The direction of the sunlight has emphasized the poppy and enhanced the contrasts of colour.

A camera club competition award winner.

OM-1   Eklachrome 64   50mm lens   1/125th sec @ f8.

interest perhaps in the form of hands, a strengthening feature can be added to the arrangement.

Carvings, heavily grained woodwork, architectural features and statues are further examples where emphasizing certain detail can be rewarding. Oblique lighting is superior for accentuating texture and for defining rough surfaces. A good plan is to keep any arrangement basically simple, ensuring that the subject is well illuminated, so that the finished print displays detail which is sharp and the principal object satisfactorily reproduced. A well-composed print of specific architectural detail in close up will make a stronger presentation than a picture showing an entire building in the middle distance.

Holidays

The pleasure which can be derived from taking photographs while on holday is shown in the large number of entries which are submitted to the many holiday picture contests. Beaches, parks and fairgrounds provide numerous opportunities for enjoyable photography; a toddler eating candy floss, grandfather asleep in a deckchair, or children emerging from the helter-skelter slide. All these are holiday moments which can be adequately recorded on film to provide delightful shots of possible competition standard.

With so many entries and with some depicting similar subjects, it is obvious that the pictures which contain something more than a mere record will secure the judges' recognition. An unusual perspective of rock formation, a dramatic shot of swimmers or against-the-light pictures of springboard divers, are the types of subject treatment from which competition photographs can be found and which provide the required impact to contend successfully with the hundreds and often thousands of entries.

For beach scenes, the bright light will enable the use of a fast shutter speed to arrest the action of ball games, people jumping over breakwaters and antics in the sea. Informal portraits on the beach which are shot at mid-day when the sun is overhead can cause heavy facial shadows, but these can be lessened by fill-in flash or by reflecting light into the shadow areas with a towel or newspaper.

Endeavour to isolate your subject, especially if the beach is crowded. Confused backgrounds can be avoided by shooting from a low angle. Use the sea and sky as a backcloth but remember to keep the horizon level. Always make use of lobster pots, fishing boats, sand dunes or anything which will inject atmosphere into the picture.

To make a picture of children digging sand more dramatic get in close and down to ground level. Shots of youngsters splashing in the water can be given extra impact by being produced in silhouette. Although facial expressions will be lost, by exposing for the sky, the figures will appear as bold dark shapes set against a sparkling sea. An ultra violet filter will protect your lens from sea spray, a lens hood will reduce flare, and a supply of polythene bags will be useful for keeping your equipment free from sand. Always load film into your camera in the shade and if possible away from the beach.

Many of the shots taken at the seaside reveal the common fault of the photographer standing too far from the activity. Although a subject which is too small in the picture area can be enlarged at the printing stage, beyond a certain point quality will deteriorate because of over-enlargement. The best policy is to 'make' your picture at the time you expose the film and to get as near as possible to the subject. Moving in close eliminates the numerous distracting

'Fun of the Fair': Another way of depicting the fairground activity would have been to employ a slow shutter speed and used blur as an indication of movement. On this occasion I preferred to freeze the action featuring the flower-like appearance of the structure and including the fun-fair enthusiasts enjoying their ride.
   Certificate in a Domesday Project national photographic contest.

OM-1 Kodachrome 64 75-150mm zoom 1/125th sec @ f8.

details which compete with the image and often lose points in competition reckoning.

Do not overlook the possibilities of still life shots which exist at the seaside. Patterns formed in the sand by the tide can be very effective when photographed against the light, especially when the sun is low and emphasis can be given to ripples and the texture of the sand. There should never be a shortage of themes or subject matter. Seaweed, pebbles and rocks can be used as the centre of interest or in a supporting role as natural props for pictures which are different from the average shots taken at the seaside. An additional advantage is that the best kind of light for still life pictures on the beach is at the start and close of the day when the beaches are not crowded with holiday makers.

The sea shore can yield a profusion of pictures, each one different according to the lighting and time of day. Set yourself an assignment of capturing on film the various moods of the sea over a period of a

'Low Tide': The repetition of the breakwater shapes created an overall appearance of design. The two young people provided a necessary point of interest. I would have preferred the figures to have been slightly separated, but had to make the most of the situation. The little white-topped wave completed the composition.

This picture won the supreme award for the colour transparency of the year in an annual camera club exhibition.

OM-1   Kodachrome 64   75-150mm zoom   1/125th sec @ f8.

'Moorings': This is the style of picture which is often seen at photographic society and club exhibitions. The design activity of the photograph is derived from the curving sweeps of the ropes and chains, leading from the darkened wall to the beach and deserted boats, which command attention by position and colour.

A camera club award winner.

Exa 500   Ektachrome   50mm lens   1/125th sec @ f5.6.

week. While making a serious approach in this way try to express yourself in an individual style as you endeavour to convey the sea in a serene or dramatic way.

When you visit an area noted for a viewpoint where the majority of tourists take a picture, make an extra effort to discover different angles or try the varied lighting conditions that early morning or evening can provide. Some beauty spots have been photographed so many times that any pictures which depict the well-known scenes have to be very exceptional in order to win a competition.

Never lose a chance of taking photographs of local people and their crafts and try to portray the atmosphere of their environment at the same time. During the summer months festivals, carnivals and village fetes present many ideas for pictures. Market days in country areas are always full of interest and can generate inspiration for unusual shots.

'A Master Thatcher': This is the sort of subject which would be suitable for competitions requesting pictures of crafts and customs which are sometimes announced in county magazines or sponsored by a company nationally. Such competitions usually have more than one category and have sections comprising contemporary and traditional themes.
Runner-up in a Country Crafts competition.

OM-1   Kodachrome 64   75-150mm zoom   1/125th sec @ f5.6.

Countryside holidays are quieter by comparison, nevertheless, a variety of situations such as rambling, farmyard activity and harvesting will provide innumerable occasions for photography. Here again judicious use of surroundings, farm buildings, hayricks, tractors and gates will give authenticity and help to set the mood of your pictures. Camping and all the activity that goes with it presents further variations of the holiday theme.

A competition for holiday photographs embraces a wide range of subjects ranging from a small child with bucket and spade to a picture of a vast mountain range. Although diverse in content both pictures are the kind which qualify for the holiday subject classification.

However, it is the inclusion of human activity and interest that often wins the day. Usually, landscapes or general scenes have to be of exceptional quality to obtain awards in an open competition. But do not let that deter you where holiday pictures are concerned. Continue to photograph and submit landscape and travel pictures but keep a lookout for subject matter depicting leisure pursuits such as horse riding, dinghy sailing and rock climbing. Competition pictures should show something of the adventurous or exotic aspects of a holiday.

Do not let the carefree holiday atmosphere affect your photography and cause you to take pictures haphazardly. Although the scenery may be unfamiliar and therefore very impressive, it does not mean that successful photography will automatically happen. You will still need to exercise the same skill that is required when taking shots of the most mundane subject.

Holiday time means photographic memories for the family album, but with attention to composition and an eye for the spontaneous event, even the so-called holiday record shot can aspire to competition standard.

A holiday in a strange environment is not the time to try out new equipment nor a different brand of film. Neither is it advisable to experiment with a newly acquired technique, it is preferable to try out anything new in local surroundings where shots can be repeated should the results be unsatisfactory.

Humour

To capture humour on film one must always be ready to recognize something that is amusing or funny in an ordinary situation. Humour usually involves people so it is a feature which can be found in the human interest side of photography.

If you see an incident which suggests a measure of humour take a shot immediately in the same manner as you would record a candid picture. If the happening or the humour continues, check your camera settings and try to improve the composition before taking further shots. When you are confronted with a brief one-off incident, remember that picture arrangement and accurate exposure come second to getting an unrepeatable picture.

Some of the funniest photographs are those which have been seen and recorded by the photographer in everyday circumstances, which endorses the suggestion that you should always carry a camera. When you do go out looking for pictures, set yourself an assignment of shooting a series of humorous incidents.

If you have an outstanding idea but find it impossible to incorporate the set-up in one picture, a photo-montage could be the answer. It will involve cutting out figures and objects from more than one photograph, then pasting them on to a master

'Tail of Temptation': A short break in the carnival procession enabled one of the bands to rest for a few moments, just in front of my kerbside position. I was facing the direction of the little boy when he suddenly raised his hand to touch the tail hanging behind the bandsman. I immediately focused the lens and pressed the shutter release. Before I had an opportunity to improve the composition in the viewfinder, the lad was pulled back to the kerb by his parent. The entire accident had been concluded as quickly as it had started, and I was left wondering whether I had captured the moment on film. The result indicated I had—just, but it would have been so much better if I could have taken another shot showing the boy's hand more clearly.
Camera club award winner.

Rolleiflex T   Ilford FP4   75mm lens   1/250th sec @ f8

'Big Heads': A shot taken while watching a carnival procession in which the humorous content was already established by the three participators wearing larger-than-life heads. Backgrounds can be very troublesome especially if you want to isolate a group from the remainder of the procession. In the short time that is usually available to take a picture, one of the best methods is to try to fill the frame with the subject.
Cash prize-winner in *Tit-Bits* magazine 'Summer Special' photographic competition.

Rolleiflex T   Ilford FP3   75mm lens   1/125th sec @ f11

photograph. Much will depend on the type of subject you choose, but if done with care, it can be a very effective method of presenting humour.

A montage photograph which is funny, often depends on the reproduction of objects, people and buildings in reduced or exaggerated scale, which because of the incredulity of the images, appears amusing. In other words you actually create your own humorous situation.

The montage must be carefully planned. By drawing a rough layout to scale you can work out the most pleasing composition. For example, if you were working on an idea to portray a fisherman struggling with an enormous fish at the end of his line, you would first require a basic picture of a fisherman and line. The second step would be to enlarge a picture of a fish to an exaggerated size. The fish would be cut out with a surgical scalpel blade and the cut-out edges chamfered with extra fine sandpaper to obviate any hard shadows when the cut-out is fixed to the master print. Any edges or joins which appear too obvious can be retouched with a spotting medium before the montage is rephotographed in order to produce a negative for the final pictures. Always ensure that a camera is square on to a montage and as close as focusing permits. You might be able to use old pictures from your file but if you do, make certain that the subject matter of the prints to be combined as a montage is illuminated from the same angle, and that the grain is of a similar size.

Humour differs according to the individual. A picture which can be uproariously funny to one viewer might be only mildly amusing to another. Sometimes in camera club circles a judge will laugh at a humorous entry, comment favourably and speak of the value of humour in photography, but when it comes to handing out the awards, the humorous shot is overlooked. This is a chance one takes when submitting humour in an ordinary competition. The criterion is whether the photograph is funny enough to have general appeal, provided of course, that the picture is technically good too.

When producing a photograph especially for a competition with humour as the set theme it will be helpful to make a list of your initial ideas, then after further consideration select two or three which can be advanced to the camera stage. For this type of subject, entries will vary depending on the photographer's interpretation of the theme. Competitors might be requested to enter photographs conforming to categories such as 'Holiday humour', or 'Humour in the home'.

Successful pictures will be those which depict spontaneity, so one must be careful that a planned humorous picture does not appear to be contrived. This can be apparent when adults and children are dressed-up in a comical way. Even though the result is likely to be of great amusement to the family or person concerned, such humour is not usually suitable for photographic contests.

The same considerations apply to the 'hall of mirrors' type of photograph which shows people distorted into ridiculously funny shapes and sizes. Such pictures are excellent for spreading mirth in family albums, but need to be something really outstanding to gain an award in a competition.

An image can be deliberately distorted in the darkroom by curling the printing paper at the enlarging stage. When using this method the enlarging lens should be stopped down to a small aperture.

The humorous content of some photographs is so apparent that a title is needless. In other instances, where the humour is subtle, an apt or explanatory title is required to direct the viewer to the meaning of the picture. An amusing title or caption can always help in confirming the humour of a picture, but a title should never be used in the hope of transforming an ordinary photograph into a humorous one.

With all the astute pre-planning possible, there is nothing to beat the humorous situation which occurs naturally. One should always be alert to such instances and capitalize on any opportunity. Incidents such as a small boy, oblivious to everyone, trying to march in step alongside a military band or the bored expressions of youngsters as they watch their parents'

enjoyment in trying out their children's new toys. Carnival processions too, can be a source of ideas, from the performed humour of the clowns and participants to the many impromptu happenings which occur on such occasions.

Humour takes many forms and can sometimes be derived from signs which display instructions or warnings and can be read as something quite different from the message which was intended. Humour can also be seen through the proximity of two notice boards, individially showing an ordinary statement, but by being viewed together proving to be extremely funny, especially if you can include someone in the picture with a perplexed expression.

There are competitions which include a section for humour or offer a prize for the funniest entry, these are the sort of contests to look for if humour is your strong point.

Landscapes and Seascapes

For successful landscape and seascape photography always remember that the camera does not view things in the same way as our eyes. Invariably the impressiveness of a scene is due to the vast distance over which the human eye can scan. For this reason the breathtaking views of woodland areas or the patchwork pattern of sundrenched meadows can result in mediocre pictures. A distant ocean liner can become an insignificant image when photographically reproduced.

A main point of interest is essential in a landscape or seascape picture, so eliminate anything that is unnecessary to the composition. A boat or person situated in an appropriate position can transform an otherwise lifeless view, but care should be taken that human interest does not dominate the scene.

With seascapes it is not always possible to change your viewpoint easily, especially if you happen to be standing by the water's edge trying to cope with a rocky coastline which is in shadow and a beach which is bright with strong sunlight. In such situations one answer is to change the lens to one of a different focal length, another solution would be to settle for a compromise in the arrangement of the picture. In the circumstances described the exposure would also need careful attention because of the strong contrast.

When using black-and-white film for seascapes, excessive contrast can be eased at both the developing and printing stages when a measure of correction can be made. If most or all the frames on a film are to be exposed in high contrast conditions over-expose your film by approximately two stops and then subsequently reduce development by a third. The negatives will then be of lower contrast as a result of the highlight and shadow areas being brought closer together. The use of a softer grade of printing paper will also achieve a better result from a contrasty negative. High contrast in colour negative film cannot be compensated in the same way because of likely changes in the colour balance.

When shooting pictures of harbours many features will catch your eye as a possible point of interest; boats, ropes, lobster pots, nets and all the paraphernalia that makes a harbour scene alive and colourful for a photographer. The problem in such surroundings is that one can be overwhelmed by the appeal of the locality and include too much in the frame. Take an overall view for record purposes but then be drastic in leaving out anything which is superfluous. Ensure that the subject matter you have selected as the focal point is in a prominent position, with the secondary shapes and lines contributing to the composition in a subservient role.

Whereas harbours and similar scenes can suffer from an overcrowding of interest, some areas of landscapes can be difficult to convey creatively because of a flat appearance. Distant views require foreground interest which can relate to the overall area. This can be achieved by including a gate or fence as a foreground element. A tree can be used as a frame or if the branches and foliage are suitable, as a lead-in to an appropriate middle distance focal point.

Unless you have a specific reason, try to avoid dividing a landscape into equal halves by having the horizon in the middle of the print. It is generally preferable to place the horizon a third of the way from the top or bottom edge of the picture. A photographer can exert considerable control over a scene, simply by a shrewd choice of viewpoint. Always seek alternative picture arrangements by composing the scene in the viewfinder from as many different angles as possible before deciding on the camera position.

Ploughed furrows, hedgerows and paths are natural lines which give design to a picture. Clusters of trees provide shape and can give perspective and depth. Landscapes can be reproduced as peaceful and serene or rugged and windswept, with the success of the final print dependent to a large extent on the prevailing lighting conditions. Even so, one can take advantage of interesting skyscapes by selecting filters to render cloud formations to the best advantage. An orange filter will always give dramatic emphasis by darkening a blue sky. Although an exciting sky will enrich a competently photographed landscape or seascape, it will not necessarily transform a mediocre composition into prizewinning quality. By the same reasoning a filter will never convert a poor picture arrangement into one of exhibition standard, but its effect will enhance a good photograph. One of the most popular filters for landscapes is a yellow-green with a x2 exposure factor. The advantages are that it darkens blue sky and at the same time lightens green foliage.

Landscape photography should be practised throughout the year in order to take advantage of each season's variations in lighting and atmosphere. The bleaker days should not be overlooked. Bare trees

'Evening Light': The purpose of the composition was to use the splendour of the tree, which had been enhanced by the evening sun, and contrast it to the man-made bridge in the background. As the structure was dwarfed by the tree's dominant position in the frame it was imperative that the bridge should be defined as clearly as possible. This was achieved partly by the dark tone of the overshadowing mountain and by careful printing at the enlarging stage.

Exhibited a number of times including East Anglian Federation, Essex International Salon of Photography and a trophy winner in a camera club exhibition.

Bronica S2A   Ilford FP4   75mm lens (yellow filter)   1/125th sec @ f11

and the stark countryside of winter can be effectively conveyed by contrasting the darker shapes against lighter toned areas and frost-covered ground.

Misty days can provide pictures with a difference, especially when the sun is beginning to break through, giving a soft subdued light. Do not take photographs to record only the overall effect of mist, but use the mist to create mood and abstract images.

Autumn foliage can be considered as a bonus to the landscape photographer. As the trees lose their leaves, the branches become exposed and therefore more

Opposite page, top: 'Furrows': Moving in to concentrate on the furrows has given the picture a sense of design. The low sun enforces not only the diagonal lines but it also strengthens the tree and bales which occupy strong positions in the pattern, which flows from the bottom left corner to the top right of the picture. A zoom lens enabled precise framing to be employed, eliminating distracting detail for maximum effect.

Competition prize in *SLR Camera* magazine. Accepted by Nottingham National Open Exhibition and Rushden Open Colour Slide Exhibition.

OM-1   Kodachrome 64   71-150mm zoom   1/60th sec @ f5.6

Opposite page, bottom: 'Landshapes': The attraction of the photograph is in the arrangement of the shapes, the ploughed section being the dominant aspect. Those who like a lead-in, especially in landscape photographs, will note the wall starting from the lower left and 'leading' the eye to the white gate, then to the ploughed area and the tractor which retains a strong position in the arrangement. Pictures of shapes and design are an alternative approach when considering landscape competitions.

Award winner in a camera club exhibition.

OM-1   Kodachrome 64   75-150mm zoom   1/125th sec @ f5.6

suitable to be incorporated as a focal point of the picture. Autumn tints are ideal for colour film with the subtle tones providing an exciting array. Black and white film can be used successfully with back lighting which enhances grassland and hedgerows. Shooting against the light gives exceptional luminosity to translucent leaves and bright surfaces. Whereas with landscape photography in the summer, one can usually return on another occasion, autumn pictures have to be recorded promptly, particularly when strong winds can cause a tree to shed its leaves very rapidly.

Below: 'Mellow Impression': Colourful sunrises and sunsets are spectacular subjects that very few photographers have not tried to capture on film. There are also worthwhile occasions when the sun is about to disappear behind a mountain or trees when the quality of light bathes the landscape with a soft ethereal beauty which transforms distant hills and foliage to a background of delicate shades of colour.

Camera club competition winner.

OM-1   Kodachrome 64   75-150mm zoom   1/60th sec @ f5.6

Opposite page, top: **'Winter':** Snow can transform the most mundane scene into an area of sparkling beauty. Shooting into the weak winter sunshine has emphasized the shadows of the disturbed snow and given texture to the frozen pond. An orange filter was used to give colour to a pale sky and accentuate the glow of the sun.
Camera club award winner.

OM-1   Kodachrome 64   28mm lens (85c filter)   1/125th sec @ f5.6

Opposite page, bottom: **'First Fall':** A colour transparency, which apart from the subtle colour on the trees, could have been taken on black-and-white film. In either medium, snow will simplify shapes and objects and replace detail with its own covering of texture. Any monotony in the overall whiteness of the scene has been balanced by the attractive shapes of the trees. Snow is a powerful reflector so a lens hood was essential for this shot.
A camera club exhibition award winner.

OM-1   Kodachrome 64   50mm lens   1/125th sec @ f8

Above: **'Snowdonia Sunset':** Just before the sun became lost behind the mountain range, the last rays were highlighting the two parallel lines in the lower right of the frame. To exaggerate the sunset effect, I employed an orange contrast filter, normally used for black-and-white photography. A zoom lens was set at 150mm to give a telephoto effect of apparent compression of the distant mountains.
£150 prize in a national Holiday Photograph Competition. Exhibited at Essex International Salon of Photography.

OM   Kodachrome 64   75-150mm zoom (orange filter) 1/125th sec @ f5.6

Snow, ever attractive to the photographer, can provide the basis for compelling and dramatic pictures, particularly when complemented by sunlight, which imparts sparkle, defines texture and usually promotes pictorial quality. With snow it is very easy to fall into the trap of recording a scene because of its unusual appearance and overlook the aspects of composition.

Although a familiar landscape which is considered mediocre can be transformed by an attractive cloak of snow to a picturesque scene, it does not automatically elevate the picture to a prize-winning category. One must be objective and select locations which are

'A Summer's Day': In landscape photography it is beneficial to hold the tone of a blue sky, either to emphasize white clouds or to maintain some tone in a cloudless sky. A yellow filter will achieve this, but when a stronger separation is required an orange filter is the next choice. 'A Summer's Day' has succeeded because the clouds have been accentuated as an important element and have complemented the foreground shape of the beach. In addition to a number of acceptances in exhibitions it was included in a portfolio of pictures which obtained the 'Photographer of the Month' award in *SLR Camera* magazine.

Bronica S2A   Ilford FP4 (orange filter)   75mm lens   1/125th sec @ f8

already strong in subject matter and to which snow provides an additional dimension.

Oblique lighting is a prerequisite for the texture of snow to be reproduced in its true sparkling crispness.

With the overall whiteness and high reflectance of snow care should be taken to avoid under exposure, which can be the cause of grey looking snow in the finished photograph.

Colour film can provide a distinctive element to a snow scene, such as a pedestrian wearing a colourful coat in an otherwise deserted area, but it can bring problems too, especially when snow is photographed beneath a clear blue sky which results in a strong blue cast. Colour casts can be reduced when a colour print is made, but with colour reversal film, once the transparency has been taken little can be done. Therefore any remedial action must be carried out at the camera stage by using a colour correcting filter. Sometimes it is preferable to retain some blueness in snow scenes to convey the impression of coldness.

Generally the most successful landscape and seascape pictures which are entered for competitions are those in which lines, shapes and tones combine in leading the eye to the principal part of the composition. At times it may be necessary to sacrifice detail to improve the overall effect, especially with sunset shots when shapes in silhouette are vital to the overall presentation.

A sunset can transform an ordinary setting into a scene of spectacular colour and is a very popular subject for competitions. The impact of a landscape at sunset will always be increased by attractive cloud formations. Seascapes too, can be vastly improved if additional interest, such as a boat, can be included in the picture when the sun is low.

Night Scenes

Photography at night is both fascinating and rewarding in the variety of strong interest pictures that are obtainable. Seaside promenades, buildings, streets and statues are dramatically transformed when floodlit. Obviously a tripod is a valuable accessory for time exposures, but a window ledge or wall can be a useful substitute provided you fire the shutter with a cable release. It must be remembered that during a time exposure the headlights of passing vehicles will record as ribbons of light. Unless you wish to include the car lights for effect they can be eliminated by shielding the lens with a piece of card until the traffic has passed by.

In practice there is more tolerance with night-time exposures but it is better to be generous rather than err on the side of under exposure. Experience will indicate that the length of exposure will largely depend on the amount of shadow detail you wish to retain. Until you are familiar with photography after dark, bracket your exposure times, i.e., one stop over and one stop under the meter reading in addition to the recommended exposure time.

In low lighting conditions taking an exposure reading can be extremely difficult when using a camera with a built-in meter which gives exposure information in the viewfinder. Some hand-held meters have a button which will lock the meter pointer in place, which enables you to read the exposure information by the light of a pocket torch without influencing the meter settings. A small torch can also be useful for adjusting camera controls or even as a light source to focus on in dim conditions.

A locking type cable release is very useful for long exposures when the camera is on the 'B' setting. If at any time you are without a tripod or cable release and you require exposures of up to one second, the delayed action timer on your camera is an excellent means of avoiding camera shake, which can be just as ruinous to your pictures at dusk as during the day. Simply place your camera on a firm support and use the delayed action timer to release the shutter.

Longer exposures will enable you to use a small aperture and therefore a larger depth of field, which is an important factor for night-time photography when

'By Day and Night': The aim of the photograph was to depict the same scene but with the different aspects of day and night. It was very important for both shots to be taken from the same viewpoint so that correct proportions could be maintained. The two negatives were combined at the printing stage with the night negative being reversed and exposed with the emulsion side facing the enlarger lamp. This was done so that the after dark scene would appear as a mirror image of the daylight scene.

Runner-up award in *Good Photography* **magazine competition.**

Rolleiflex T   Ilford FP3   75mm lens
Day: 1/125th sec @ f11
Night: 1 sec @ f5.6

it is difficult to distinguish objects for focusing purposes clearly in the view-finder.

When photographing a floodlit building avoid including a strong light or a street lamp in the foreground, otherwise it will take attention from the remainder of the scene. The inclusion of water will always enhance a night shot and inject additional atmosphere, but waves and ripples will not be too apparent in the final print as they tend to flatten out during a time exposure.

An effective way to record buildings is to

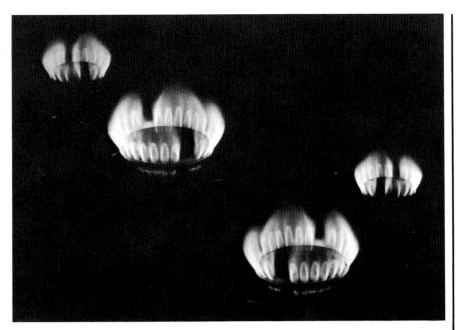

'Candlelight': A colour transparency which was the result of an attempt at a set-subject competition of after-dark photography. With low illumination such as candlelight, exposure times are difficult to determine. For this shot a hand-held meter was used. A reflective surface was placed behind the candle to provide a secondary area of colour to balance the light of the flame.

A winning entry in a camera club exhibition.

OM-1 Kodachrome (Type A) 50mm lens 1/15th sec @ f4.

'Power Flowers': The picture was made by sandwich printing. Two negatives were combined and exposed simultaneously at the enlarging stage. One negative was reversed left to right in order to achieve the composition. When the print was selected at a District Arts Association awards for photography exhibition, the published comments of the judge were, "From a mundane subject, the photographer has conceived a good association of ideas which results in a picture of good design and technical execution, neatly tied together by a clever title."

In addition to being selected for the East Anglian Federation Exhibition the print was selected to represent the EAF in the Photographic Alliance of Great Britain Inter-Federation competitions.

Rolleiflex T Ilford FP4 75mm lens approx. 5 secs @ f5.6

photograph them at lighting-up time while there is still tone in the sky. This avoids the kind of result which shows only the illuminated windows. Instead the outline and shape of the building is depicted as well, which gives depth to your photograph. For an out-of-the-ordinary shot you can take the method a step further by double exposure. It is essential to use a tripod and ensure the camera position is identical for each shot. Make your first exposure at dusk to record detail and basic shapes, then once it is dark make your second exposure on the same frame. This technique can be very successful for seaside illuminations.

When shooting colour at night you have the choice of using daylight film which will give a warm result with any white subjects taking on a yellow appearance or you can use a tungsten balanced film which will give a colder but more accurate rendering. Alternatively you can convert daylight film with a blue filter (80A) which of course will necessitate ad-

ditional exposure.

No reference to night photography would be complete without consideration of fireworks. Undoubtedly a firework display provides exceptional opportunities for colour and black and white. A tripod is necessary and careful choice of viewpoint important. Unless they are very special, pictures of individual fireworks are not usually impressive. For eye-catching pictures it means employing the technique of keeping the shutter open to record multiple images of bursts of colour or exploding rockets. For this type of picture it is advisable to keep the camera at a reasonable distance from the display, otherwise some fireworks will cascade outside the picture area. Imaginative photographs can be produced when a firework display takes place by a lake or river which enables you to include colourful reflections and abstract patterning in the water.

Although the idea is not new, a picture of a

youngster holding a sparkler in each hand has a number of variations and usually provides an exciting November-the-fifth celebration shot. Lightning can also be photographed by opening the shutter on a time setting and allowing several flashes to be recorded on the same piece of film.

You should never have difficulty in finding subject matter. For a start your first location could be the nearest street lamp from where you live or even in your own home. The most mundane building can sparkle with life by the illumination of after dark lighting. The effect is further increased after a shower which causes wet roads and pavements to glisten as lights are reflected upon the wet surfaces. The earlier you can start shooting after it has been raining the more variations of reflection-pictures should be possible. Special effect filters such as cross-screen and starburst can also give a night shot the extra brilliance that is necessary to be successful in competition photography.

Fairgrounds are ideal for atmosphere and pictures

'Mont Orgueil Castle': Having photographed the castle earlier in the day I was astonished to see the impact floodlighting had made to the castle and row of buildings. Not anticipating any night photography and not carrying a tripod it was necessary to improvise and use a wooden box to support the camera. A cable release was also used to reduce the risk of camera shake. It is always encouraging after photographing certain pictures with difficulty to discover when the films are processed that perseverance was worthwhile.

The print won a runner-up award of a plaque and £10 in the Ilford FP4 Challenge Cup Competition and a £10 second prize in a Jersey Tourism Photographic Contest.

Rolleiflex T   Ilford FP4   75mm lens   approx. 5 secs @ f5.6

taken after-dark seem to convey the excitement much better than daytime shots. Most funfairs provide a variety of situations which are challenging to the photographer who is willing to try alternative methods. The big wheel is always a colourful spectacle and lends itself to time exposures for unusual effects. Always take a new exposure meter reading when you move from one sideshow to another.

The fact that a picture happened to be taken after dark is not sufficient reason for submitting a night shot to an open competition which has no set theme. Although your picture might be the only night shot entered, it must contain a quality which will impress the judges. Interest can be injected into an after-dark shot by careful focusing at maximum aperture so that lights in the background can appear as out-of-focus patterns and shapes.

Castles take on a cloak of grandeur when floodlit and make excellent subjects in colour and black-and-white. Usually the positioning of the floodlights emphasizes the important features of the structure and this contributes immensely to picture arrangement as well as providing a centre of interest. Churches too, benefit from lighting of this sort. It is always advisable to take exposure readings from as close to the buildings as possible.

Town centres with illuminated pedestrian precincts and shop windows bathed in light are further ideas for night shots. Shop window displays are usually bright enough to make a tripod unnecessary. Neon lighting displays also provide after-dark features. The illuminated advertisements are not only colourful and attractive but are also suitable for a variety of techniques. If the adjacent pavements are wet, reflected areas of colour can be very effective, especially if you can position the camera so that a dominant feature or colour is mirrored in a puddle. Neon lighting is also suitable for multi-exposures for uncommon effects. The key factor when taking more than one shot on the same frame is to remember the position of the areas of colour on the previous exposure.

Portraits

Competitions for portraiture are generally found in photographic magazines; exhibitions too, include a section for this specialized branch of photography.

Any portrait should be a pleasing representation of the sitter and depict good characterization as well as being a satisfactory composition. Pictures for competitions should attain a standard which has a broader appeal than the conventional portrait which is taken for personal and family interest.

When attempting portraiture for the first time, it is possible to be so involved with technical matters, that mannerisms and expressions, which can be split-second happenings, are often missed. In this respect outdoor portraiture can be less demanding for the beginner. Apart from the choice of background, attention can be devoted to posing the model.

Before starting any portrait session the photographer must have a definite idea of results to aim for and

'Night Duty': This picture has been commended for its atmosphere, which the table lamp illumination helps to establish. The dark surrounding areas direct attention to the nurse and her relationship with the items on the desk. This is an example of the sort of approach and coverage of a subject which is successful in competitions between photographic societies and clubs.

The picture has been selected to represent the East Anglian Federation in the Photographic Alliance of Great Britain Inter-Federation Competitions. Also accepted by the Rushden Open Colour Slide Exhibition.

Zenith E   Ektachrome 160 (Tungsten)   58mm lens   1/30th sec @ f5.6

an idea of how to achieve them. Camera and accessories should be checked beforehand and a list made of details concerning subject arrangement, areas of background to avoid and any filters to be used.

'Royal Guard': A candid portrait of a subject which attracted my attention because of its bold colour, particularly the strong splash of red set against the area of shadow. Diffused light is usually preferred for colourful clothing but on this occasion the harsh sunlight has given a clarity and emphasis to the uniform without 'burning out' the detail on the helmet.
Selected for the East Anglian Federation Exhibition.

Olympus FTL   Kodachrome   50mm lens   1/125th sec @ f5.6

'Outdoor Portrait': An informal portrait in which the restful background importantly conveys the mood of a pleasant summer's day. The theme is continued in the complementary colours of the headscarf and blouse. It is always important to give attention to colours of accessories in portraits, even in an informal outdoor shot such as this, when one inappropriate item can spoil the effect.
A camera club exhibition award.

Rolleiflex T   Ektachrome 64   75 mm lens   1/125th sec @ f5.6

A very important factor is that from the moment your model arrives, put him or her at ease and start a conversation. Continue to talk while making adjustments to the camera or when taking exposure readings. Your aim should be to get your model to feel and look relaxed and to appear natural in the subsequent photographs.

As you try to capture an aspect of a person's character, get to know their interests and then make them a point of conversation. Sometimes appropriate

music, played softly, assists in creating a relaxed atmosphere.

For outdoor portraits a hazy sun is preferable to the harsher glare of bright sunlight, which makes heavier shadows and can cause the sitter to frown and squint. The stronger the light the more necessary it will be to lighten the shadows. A sheet of white paper or card will make an efficient reflector for softening the shadow areas. An alternative to a reflector is the method of using fill-in-flash from a small flashgun.

First the camera is set at a speed recommended for flash, and the lens aperture is adjusted to give the correct exposure according to the lighting conditions. The flash guide number should be increased by half and divided by the aperture setting. The result of the calculation will be the flash-(not the camera) to-subject distance in feet, and will provide sufficient fill-in light to soften the shadow areas. A flash extension lead will probably be required and the covering of the flashgun with a handkerchief will reduce the light further if necessary.

For a head and shoulders portrait, unless you have a good reason for not doing so, try to place the head above centre in the picture, so that it assumes a strong position. If the hands are to be included they should make a definite contribution to the composition.

For anyone who has taken portraits outdoors only,

'Pastor': Taking pictures of people is one of the most popular subjects of photography. Evidence of this can be seen in family albums, magazines and also among photographic societies who organize studio groups and place portrait sessions high on the programme of their activities. There are numerous ways of lighting a person for a portrait. The illumination can be flash or provided by one lamp or several, with no technique or method considered to be the proper way. The lighting arrangement for this shot comprised three lamps with one of them directed on to a projection screen which was used as a background.

The picture gained first award in a camera club portrait competition.

Rolleiflex T   Ilford FP4   75mm lens   1/15th sec @ f8

the next step is to attempt indoor portraiture by daylight. Excellent pictures can be achieved with the minimum of equipment. By posing the sitter near a window, available light can be utilized with the addition of a white card as a reflector for filling in the inevitable shadows. A large mirror is also useful in this respect. Kitchen baking foil can be used but in some situations it gives rather harsh reflections. Foil manufactured for photographic purposes can be purchased in various surface colours including gold, which is particularly useful for special effects when you are shooting in colour. Use a reflector in the same way as an extra lamp.

Although window lighting is a soft light source, it functions as the main modelling light, which you control by altering the sitter's position until the desired effect is obtained. An important point is not to place your model too close to the window otherwise the contrast between light and shadow will be too great. An uncurtained window is ideal, but depending on the effect you are trying to capture, it is worth experimenting with diffusing the light through net curtains or venetian blinds. Do not use a window which has direct sunlight shining through, but choose a window which will transmit good even illumination. A cloudy bright sky gives the best light.

Artificial lighting can be provided by flash (see Chapter Two) or photofloods. Ordinary household lamps are not really bright enough for indoor photography and although photofloods appear to be similar to household bulbs, they are specially made to give extra light. The No.1 size consumes 275 watts but gives approximately 600 watts light output and lasts for about two hours. A No.2 photoflood gives double the amount of light, uses twice as much current and lasts for about eight hours.While arranging your model, you can conserve the life of the photofloods by using a series-parallel distribution board and switching the lights to half power. Photoflood lamps get extremely hot and should not be used in domestic lampshades but only in metal reflectors.

With a basic three lamp set-up it is worthwhile to experiment with the positioning of the lamps, noting the different effects of light and shadow which can be created. Start by setting the main light at an angle of about 45° to a line between the camera and the sitter, and about two feet higher than eye level. Too many shadows should be avoided. Lamp two can be positioned as a fill-in light near the camera, but at a distance which is farther away than lamp one. The third lamp can be used to illuminate the background.

If a sheet is used for a background ensure that any creases or folds are ironed out. Alternatively a projection screen can provide a plain background which can be easily adjusted according to the position of your sitter.

A good portrait should suggest something of the model's character. A contemporary technique of

'Christmas': Because a picture is a competition winner it does not mean that it is beyond reproach. Although this print has won recognition over the years it suffers from a common fault of overloading. When it was first published constructive criticism printed in a magazine drew attention to the problem—that the bunch of holly on the table in the left hand corner was superfluous. It is remarkable how often we fail to see defects in our own work. That is why there is an advantage of viewing our photographs through the eyes of others. Photofloods provided the illumination. In spite of the shortcoming, the print has gained awards in *Practical Photography, Amateur Photographer,* and *International Photo Contest* magazines.

Bessa 1   Ilford FP3   1/25th sec. @ f4.5

conveying this is to relate the sitter to the background. In contrast to the conventional studio portrait the direct relevance between the model and location would be suggested in a portrait of an artist surrounded by paintings, or perhaps a farmer pictured against a background of a farm. Such photographs need to be arranged with care, even though the final result may indicate a feeling of informality.

Special Effects

Among the different kinds of photographs which are to be seen on exhibition walls and in the photographic press, are those produced by unusual techniques. One example of a special effect is the type of picture made by using a texture screen, which is combined with the negative at the enlarging stage. Other styles include the multiple-image picture in which more than one negative is used, and two-tone separation photographs which require negatives and positives of different tones to be reproduced from the original image.

For the photographer who has never attempted unusual effects a method worth trying is tone elimination in which the tones of the original continuous tone negative are converted to either black or white. The result is an ultra high contrast photograph which contains no middle tones whatever and consists of solid black and paper-base white areas only.

Anyone who has developed their own photographs should be capable of achieving high contrast pictures of abstract appearance. The most suitable negatives for this type of application are those containing bold shapes, silhouettes and prominent patterns, with the subject matter well separated from the background. Even a mediocre photograph can acquire striking impact when produced as a high contrast picture by using lith film and developer.

First, the original continuous tone negative is contact printed on to lith film by ordinary darkroom illumination. The emulsion side of the negative is placed in direct contact with the emulsion of the unexposed lith film in the same way as a normal contact print is made. After processing in a lith developer the subsequent film positive will show that the tones of the original negative are reproduced as dense black or clear film, with the middle tones having merged with either highlights or shadows, depending on the amount of exposure the film received. It is then contacted again with another sheet of lith film to produce the required negative. Occasionally it is necessary to repeat the procedure until the desired effect is obtained.

Finally, the lith negative can be enlarged and printed by your normal method, preferably on to a hard grade of paper. The technique can be utilized to give bold treatment to many subjects and to produce unusual pictures of strong appeal, in some instances derived from original negatives which, if enlarged in the normal way, would not rate a second glance.

The use of texture screens is a conventional method of producing something unusual from an ordinary negative. For it is the print that is different, as well as pleasing, which is a potential award winner. The commercially made screens are negatives of texture patterns and are probably the easiest to use and the most straightforward of the special darkroom techniques. The screen is simply placed in contact with the original negative in the enlarger carrier. Other types of screens are also obtainable and are positioned in contact with the printing paper on the enlarger baseboard. Either way, the enlarging and processing

technique is unchanged. Among the range of screens available are reticulated grain, rough linen and tweed.

Texture screens can also be put to good use in conjunction with tone elimination techniques when they can be employed to put variation in the larger blank areas. There will always be discussion, and argument too, whether special effects are an adjunct to creativity or merely a gimmick. For competitions at least, special effects should be utilized only as an additional dimension to embellish the photograph. A picture will be doomed to failure if there is indication that the unfamiliar treatment has been used for the sake of being different, especially in contests where unusual techniques are introduced with dramatic and outstanding results.

When considering anything experimental, a good test is to compare the picture which has received special treatment with a print produced from the original negative but processed normally. Then decide for yourself whether the different technique gives the extra appeal or impact desired.

Photographs which have received treatment that is different from basic processing do win competitions and gain recognition in exhibitions. Undoubtedly you will expand your photographic horizons if you try something new. Some photographers are diffident at attempting new techniques because of the additional procedures which are entailed. However, the methods already referred to are straightforward enough and can be considered as good experience for launching into something more involved, such as bas-relief, which is a picture of overall grey, with the outline of the subject in relief, which gives an engraved appearance. It is achieved by using two films of the same image, one negative and the other positive, and sandwiching them together but with the subject matter slightly out of register.

Photo-montage, tone-separation and other derivative techniques can be seen from time to time in exhibitions and magazines. Although in the minority, those which are submitted succeed because the

'Windsor Abstract': A judge, who was giving a critical appraisal of this picture asked whether the treatment was an improvement on an ordinary black and white picture of the scene. An improvement or not, it is certainly different, with the representation of the castle in the background sustaining the abstract image of the bold shapes of the soldier and the wall. But my opinion is rather biased as this was my first attempt at using lith film to produce a high contrast picture.

Exhibited at 'The British Scene' an exhibition organized by Ilford Limited and *Practical Photography* magazine. Winner of a book prize in a competition sponsored by the photographic distributors, Johnsons of Hendon.

Bessa 1   Ilford FP3   1/100th sec @ f11

treatment has been ideally suited to the subject matter.

Special effects can also be obtained by using the extensive range of creative filters which are extremely popular with users of colour film. Graduated filters are obtainable either in conventional filter mounts or are

supplied to fit a holder that screws on to the lens by means of an adapter and accepts square-shaped filters, which enables a graduated filter to be moved either up or down in relation to the image for the most pleasing effect. The filters are available in various colours and densities. The coloured part covers less than half the area of the filter, graduating from full colour at the top to clear at the bottom half.

The atmosphere of a landscape can be transformed by using a graduated filter to intensify the sky, or to balance differences in tone, and areas of colour can be accentuated and made more dramatic. The wide range of special effect filters provides many colours and variations, from cross-screen filters which give glittering effects around lights and bright images, to filters which give the impression of fog. These are the sort of accessories which can be employed creatively for producing entries for competitons. Also in the range is a multi-image filter which reproduces an image a number of times. Although the results from this type of filter can be spectacular, they are somewhat stereotyped in appearance and require originality in the choice of subject and evidence that the photographer made an important contribution to the picture in addition to the effect of the filter.

Whether you carry out the special effect when taking the picture or during the processing, never try anything for the first time if you are producing photographs for a specific competition and they cannot be repeated. Always experiment first and try to keep notes of the various stages.

It is worthwhile repeating the advice already given that whichever method or treatment is favoured, never use it merely for its effect, but ensure that in your pursuit of creativity the special effect is in harmony with the subject and the result is an enhancement of the original.

Sport

The vital ingredients of sports pictures are activity and drama. To capture them successfully, patience and practice are required in cultivating the skill of choosing the right moment to press the shutter release. With a standard lens, it is possible to get near

'Pole Vaulter': A black-and-white image reproduced on lith film as described in the section on special effects. The original negatve was quite satisfactory in depicting the activity except that telephone wires completely spoiled the picture. Contacting the negative on to lith film solved the problem and resulted in a successful image which probably would not have seen the light of day but for the telephone wires.
   Selected for Exhibition Photographic Alliance of Great Britain, and an exhibition award winner of a quantity of colour films.

Original Film:
Rolleiflex T   Ilford FP3   75mm lens   1/500th sec @ f5.6

'Off the Mark': By obtaining a good position at a local athletics meeting I was able to use a low viewpoint near the track and record the athletes as they left their starting blocks. An important point on these occasions is to try to remain completely detached from the excitement and take great care in pressing the shutter release smoothly. At sporting events there is always the problem of distracting detail in the background and areas adjacent to the action. One method of overcoming this is to keep the background out of focus. Another is to shape your picture to fit the subject as in this photograph which has been trimmed to a letter-box shape.
Exhibited at the Essex Salon of Photography

Rolleiflex T   Ilford FP3   75mm lens   1/500th sec @ f8

enough to most events in order to record the emotion and pathos which are an integral part of the sporting scene.

One approach to sporting activities is to hold the camera still and use the fastest possible shutter speed to freeze the action, but with this method you are likely to lose the appearance of dramatic movement in the final result; a racing car photographed in this way can appear to be travelling much slower than its actual speed.

Depending on the distance you are from the activity even your fastest shutter speed will not always prevent blurred images. Evidence of blur is often desirable in communicating a sense of movement and can be further emphasized to varying degrees by using a slower shutter speed. It can be remarkably effective when blur is shown in the arms or legs of an athlete.

A well-proved technique, especially for the photographing of motor sports is known as panning.

Movement in the picture is conveyed by producing a blurred background. With the shutter set at a speed between 1/60th and 1/250th of a second, the camera is moved to follow the direction of the passing car so that the vehicle is maintained in a constant position in the viewfinder. While the camera is panned in one continuous movement, the shutter is released at a pre-determined point. The result should show a sharply defined subject against a completely blurred background.

Some are put off sports photography because they do not own a variety of lenses, but by careful choice of viewpoint to suit the lens on the camera, you can adjust your photography to the limitations and advantages of the lens being used. For those with more than one lens, never use a longer focal length lens when a shorter lens would be perfectly adequate.

A wide-angle lens can be useful for dramatic shots of track events at an athletics meeting or the start of a cycle race. The so-called standard lens will prove to be a good all round lens which will cope with most situations. The 135mm or 200mm telephoto lenses are excellent for getting amongst the action and for capturing graphic shots of facial expressions and close-ups. By pre-focusing on a selected area—a goalmouth of a football pitch or the baseline of a tennis court—one can avert last second camera adjustments when the action moves within the pre-focused range.

Telephoto lenses are also ideal for maintaining sharp focus on the principal competitors with the surrounding area out of focus. This is very useful in swimming and athletics. Telephoto lenses longer than 250mm should be mounted on a tripod and are well suited to games such as cricket, where the camera is a considerable distance from the action.

A zoom lens provides the sports photographer with a choice of focal lengths and is especially useful for events where the action moves rapidly from one area to another. A zoom lens can also be employed to create an impression of dramatic movement, by using the technique of a relatively show shutter speed and firing the shutter while zooming.

It is always helpful if you are familiar with the rules of the sport you are shooting. You will then have an understanding of what is happening and boost your chances of anticipating the imminent moves in the action. Another benefit is that you are able to select the best vantage point for the picture you require. Attention to the background is also essential when you are choosing your position.

For team games, by thinking ahead, the photographer can be poised ready to release the shutter, the moment play reaches the area in focus. This is particularly important with games in which the activity flows rapidly from one end of the arena to the other. Some knowledge of the participants' characteristics can be an advantage when you are trying to achieve a picture you have planned. In an event such as motor-cycle racing, become familiar with the riders' styles as they seemingly keep to the same part of the course on each lap. Attention to points such as this can be instrumental in anticipating the right moment for exposure.

In sports where the action passes across the field of view, to arrest the movement effectively it is necessary to squeeze the shutter release a moment before the subject reaches the required position in your viewfinder.

A spectacular subject will always attract additional attention in any competition and pictures of water sports often contain that something extra which provides the impact the judges seek. Springboard diving, surfing, swimming and water-ski-ing all display the type of action that increases the possibility of outstanding shots. Telephoto lenses can transmit the feeling that the camera is right in the middle of the action.

Motor racing has always been a popular sport for photographers, providing atmosphere and excitement. Because you are seeking prize-winning pictures it does not mean you must have Grand Prix subject matter. Although it is very satisfying to photograph world class drivers, you can capture just as exciting images at lesser-known club meetings, without the problem of coping with the large crowds who support the major circuits.

The same reasoning applies to many sports including show-jumping, when you can attend local events and take photographs from a variety of viewpoints and experiment with various shutter speeds. Poor viewpoint can turn a potentially exciting shot into

'Show-jumper': Although black-and-white pictures produced from lith film will not turn a poor shot into a dramatic one, this type of image can have a very striking effect when displayed on an exhibition wall. A plus factor with this shot is that a low viewpoint has accentuated the rider and horse who have been caught at the peak of action. This is one of the benefits that comes from photographing sport at local meetings and events, where it is easier to obtain good vantage points for taking pictures than it would be at national events.

Camera club exhibition award and exhibited at East of England Show.

Rolleiflex T   Ilford FP4   75mm lens   1/500th sec @ f8

mediocrity, whereas skilful positioning of the camera can create the sort of impact upon which the competition picture thrives.

Allied with the importance of viewpoint is background, which more often than not has to be tolerated although it can be controlled and rendered out-of-focus by using a large aperture. Background can also be made to appear as a blur by employing the panning technique. By careful focusing at full aperture a telephoto lens can be valuable in making a background inconspicuous.

In the quest for a winning picture it is vital to keep your eye on the game and to be completely accustomed to your equipment. In any sport the highlight of the activity can be lost while you are fumbling with the camera. Some peaks of action are impossible to predict so it is essential to be alert and observant in every situation.

Creating Better Pictures

'Window': The old city of Jerusalem taken through a chapel window on the Mount of Olives was awarded the Supreme prize of a Thomson Holiday in the Sun for Two, in a national competition organized by SLADE—The Society of Lithographic Artists, Designers, Engravers and Process Workers. Impact and originality were the reasons given for the judging panel's choice. The Chairman of the judges, Mr. R. H. Mason MA, FBIPP, Hon. FRPS, said ''I think the overall winner shows great originality. Thousands of pictures have been taken of this view of Jerusalem but this is the first I have seen taken through a wrought-iron screen with a cross. It gives the picture an almost poignant significance. In addition, the strong contrast of the black lines of the screen against the sunlit golds and blues of the distant scene, gives a powerful impact and creates an interesting design. It is also technically excellent as a photograph.''

Olympus FTL   Ektachrome-X   50mm lens   1/125th sec @ f11

Some photographers can attribute their initial interest in serious photography to the time they became competition-minded and tried to convey subject matter more effectively. As you seek to improve your technique and strive to make consistent progress, you will not accomplish a masterpiece every time a picture is produced, but you should be rewarded with a recognisable advancement in your photography which will give you satisfaction and further incentive as a contestant.

Improving Your Technique

Devise a routine for ensuring that the camera is correctly set before exposing your film. By setting the shutter-speed, aperture and distance in the same sequence every time you take a photograph, it will become an instinctive operation. This will enable you to concentrate entirely on composing the picture.

Always frame the picture with care and eliminate extraneous detail. One of the most challenging yet difficult operations for the beginner in competition

'In the Country': Taken on an overcast day, one judge stated that it is the kind of picture that tells a story. From the old gravestones in the foreground, there is a progression for the eye to follow to the middle distance where sheep graze in an open field, then beyond to the farmhouse and hill in the distance. Taking an alternative point of view, another judge suggested that it is really two pictures combined—a graveyard and a farm—and would benefit by separating the top and lower halves.

An award winner in SLR magazine and very successful in exhibitions.

Kowa 66   Ilford FP4   85mm lens   1/60th sec @ f5.6

photography is composing the picture and knowing when the subject looks right in the viewfinder. One way of overcoming this obstacle is by taking photographs at every opportunity, bearing in mind the recommendations of subject arrangement which should never be ignored just for the sake of achieving something that is different.

It is surprising how many photographs are spoiled by telegraph poles and hoardings, when just a few paces to the left or right would have excluded them from the picture. Before pressing the shutter release ensure that you are viewing the subject in the same way as the camera lens and not simply seeing only what you want to see.

Backgrounds are far more important than is often

realized, so when the components of a picture rely on a complementary background, consideration should be given to detail which could vie for attention. When you employ the technique of selective focusing and keep only the main subject sharp against an out-of-focus background, the importance of evaluating the subject—including each corner of the viewfinder—cannot be stressed too strongly. This is especially so when using reversal film which does not permit discrepancies in picture arrangement to be rectified in the same way as with negative film. With the latter, if you have second thoughts about what should have been left out when you originally framed the subject in the viewfinder, the picture area can be altered and cropped at the printing stage.

73

Viewpoint

Avoid being so captivated by the vista that you take a number of shots from one position without considering alternative viewpoints. This applies to general photography as well as landscape. Try to avoid maintaining the same camera height for all your exposures. Instead try to visualize the finished photograph, noting how shapes nearest the camera could be strengthened by exploiting a low viewpoint or made to recede when viewed from a higher position.

Composition

When confronted by a picturesque scene, you can be tempted to step back in order to squeeze the maximum area into the viewfinder, which invariably results in an unimpressive picture. Far better to move closer and by being selective concentrate on an area in which you can emphasize certain elements of the whole. Compose your picture so there is an unmistakable point of interest by eliminating anything that does not contribute to the composition.

One can learn a great deal about composition by looking at the work of the other photographers in exhibitions, photographic books and magazines. Composition is very much a matter of individual interpretation, but an understanding of some guiding principles can be useful in picture arrangement. The maxim that you should never allow a horizon or a tree to divide your picture into equal halves is worth observing. Another is known as the rule of thirds, where the picture area is divided into nine equal areas by imaginary lines, two horizontal and two vertical, the four points where the lines intersect are considered to be the most important positions of a composition, so the principal subject or the strongest part of the picture should be placed adjacent to one of the four points.

The components of a picture should be well balanced but not symmetrical. A repetitive arrangement of tonal masses will appear lifeless, whereas a balanced dispersal of tones will contribute to the atmosphere of the picture. A large shape of light tone can be balanced by a small shape of dark tone and vice versa.

Line and Shape

Try to cultivate an awareness of line and shape. By constantly observing your surroundings in an analytical way you will be able to compose your pictures more effectively when looking at the image through your viewfinder.

The lines of a picture, that is the lines which are formed by the edge of one tone against another, should direct the viewer's eye to the principal object. Pathways or the curve of a river should also lead into the picture rather than run off the edge of the print. A continuation of small areas of light tone can have a similar deviating effect and lead the eye away from the subject.

Photography is a means of communication and expresses the passive or aggressive aspects of a scene or subject. Horizontal lines can be used to convey the tranquillity of a pastoral scene, they can also suggest a sense of stability, whereas strong vertical lines can give an impression of grandeur. A diagonal line in a picture is usually very strong compositionally and projects a sense of activity.

Any competitor who observes the fundamentals of composition has a sound basis to work from. However, equally important as established picture arrangements, are photographs which are successful because of the artistic and visual awareness of the photographer.

The principles of composition should be considered as a general guide and not something to be followed inflexibly, otherwise one's pictures will be identical in pattern instead of showing an individual interpretation for each subject. At all times the photographer should feel free to produce imaginative ideas without being restricted by a set of so-called rules. If a picture only displays maximum impact when the horizon is placed in the centre then go ahead and present the image that way. The determining standard should be that if a picture looks right then that is the arrangement to use. Similarly there are opportunities in candid and sports photography, when the split-second expression or movement is the essence of the picture, rather than concern for the rule of thirds.

'In the Valley': My first sight of the location was on a very dull day. With little chance of an improvement in the light I decided to return another day. It took two more visits to the scene before it was suitable to take some shots, and even then, only after a long wait. When the sun first broke through the clouds, the top of the mountain was bathed in light but the chapel and bridge were untouched by the sunshine. The period of waiting gave plenty of time to decide on the best composition, which resulted in placing the chapel on a point of the 'rule of thirds'. Suddenly a small patch of light rested on the chapel and the bridge with a larger splash of sunshine moving across the mountain. The brightness faded as quickly as it appeared, but the moment had been captured.

Commended award in the Essex International Salon of Photography.

Rolleiflex T   Ilford FP4   75mm lens   1/125th sec @ f11

The Quality of Light

A photograph which has pictorial attributes will always score over a straightforward record shot, and can be accomplished by a carefully selected viewpoint and, very often, by waiting for the most suitable lighting conditions to convey the right atmosphere. With these necessities a commonplace scene can be transformed into a picture of aesthetic appeal.

The quality of light is vital in any type of photography. This fact can prompt the incorrect assertion that summer is the best season for taking pictures. However, winter lighting is not always dull and flat. Misty mornings with the sun breaking through, or frost-laden shrubs glistening in early sunshine can provide sparkle and interest equal to any picture taken in the summer months.

Neither should photography in overcast conditions be dismissed, especially if you are in a locality for only a short period. Although the lighting will be soft and

'Heroes Colonnade': If there is a time of day when photographers prefer to avoid taking pictures it is at midday when the sun is directly overhead and the shadows are harsh and sometimes unflattering. Even so, there are times when perhaps you are on a touring holiday and it would be foolish not to take pictures just because it was supposed to be the 'wrong time' for photography. This was the situation with this picture, which I preferred to take rather than ignore. Judges have commented favourably on the individual column on the right of the picture which holds together the receding 'lines' of the composition.

Very successful in exhibitions including the East of England Show.

Rolleiflex T   Ilford FP4   75mm lens   1/125th sec @ f11

'Concrete Construction': An architectural picture, taken under hazy conditions, in which the subject matter is entirely different from 'Heroes Colonnade', yet the composition relies on a recession of lines in a similar way. Usually the lines of pictures are formed by one tone adjacent to another or by shadows and shapes. In this picture however the lines are physical and exist in the concrete shapes.

Camera Club exhibition award winner.

Kowa 66   Ilford FP4   85mm lens   1/125th sec @ f5.6

distant views may appear drab, an adventurous approach will be rewarded with a delicate gradation and subtle colour which is sometimes absent in photographs taken in bright sunlight. Subjects suitable for competitions can be observed in all kinds of weather and lighting, so always be ready to use your camera in any situation.

Weather conditions have a significant effect upon colour. As the light fluctuates, colours correspondingly change with a variation of hues and tints. A landscape photographed one day can convey an entirely different representation of colour the following day. A series of photographs of the same subject taken at regular intervals throughout the day will

Opposite page, top: **'Approaching Dusk':** The failing light and the subdued colours give the picture an almost monochrome appearance. The perceptible tints in the mountain range provide a pleasing balance to the boat which is the focal point of the picture. Although the boat occupies only a small area of the frame its significance is increased by being placed on the brightest area of water.
    Camera club competition award.

OM-1   Kodachrome 64   50mm lens   1/30th sec @ f5.6

Opposite page, bottom: **'Eventide':** The basic principles of composition are good guide-lines on which a photographer can develop an individual approach and style. But there are times when guide-lines can be disregarded in the pursuit of a special arrangement. Some would be dismayed about the highlight in the lower left corner and with the positioning of the sun and tree.
    The shot was awarded first prize in a club competition. Another picture taken within seconds, with the highlight and sun arranged nearer the tree, won a prize in *Photography* magazine's World of Colour competition.

OM-1   Ektachrome 64   50mm lens   1/30th sec @ f8

Right: **'Hillside Ruin':** Mountains, hills and the remains of an old building do not seem to be an appropriate mix for competition photography. However, with sunlight accentuating the surface of the slate fence, and highlighting the window area and shape of the ruin, the various components fuse together. The fence gives a decisive lead-in from the bottom left corner of the picture to the old ruin.
    Camera club competition award. Exhibited Essex International Salon of Photography.

OM-1   Kodachrome 64   50mm lens   1/60th sec @ f8

Right: **'Raindrops':** No claim for originality is being made for the idea of a picture taken through a rain-covered windscreen. Variations of the theme sometimes show clearly defined buildings and people or depict objects blurred beyond recognition. This shot was taken from a car parked in a lay-by. A feature that has bothered some judges is the inclusion of the car's bonnet.
    An award winner in a camera club competition.

OM-1   Kodachrome 64   50mm lens   1/30th sec @ f4

reveal a continuing change of colour. This is especially noticeable when photographs are taken in the morning or evening and the sun is close to the horizon. The results will show an over-red colour balance, because daylight colour films are manufactured to provide correct colour rendering when exposed to light of a colour temperature existing at noon on a clear summer's day. When the sun is high its light is white, but when it is low the blue and ultraviolet content are filtered by the earth's atmosphere which emphasizes the red glow in sunset pictures.

Most photographers cannot resist taking pictures of sunsets, but a sunset photograph must be really outstanding to win a competition. A sunset is ideal for colour film provided you can achieve something more than a record of the glowing sun. Many sunset shots are spoiled by over-exposure because the meter reading has been calculated on foreground detail instead of allowing the interest in front of the camera to be recorded in silhouette.

Obviously the sun is the key to the whole picture but consideration must be given to other important factors in a sunset photograph. It is essential to decide, for example, on the area of sea to be included or how much landscape to emphasize in silhouette. Another approach is not to include the sun in the picture area but to show the effect of the setting sun instead. Determining exposure is not always easy but a reliable method is to take a reading from an area of sky adjacent to the sun. The impact of shapes and figures in silhouette does not have to be confined to sunsets but can be exploited whenever shooting against the light.

During the summer months it is preferable to avoid taking pictures when the sun is high overhead which consequently causes very dark shadows.

Try to observe the effect of light whenever you can. Note how the appearance of areas in shadow change according to the intensity of adjacent illumination. When the sun is low, shadows are longer which means unusual shapes and composition, as well as a lower contrast of light which benefits both colour and black and white photography.

The advantages of low sunlight are improvements in detail, texture and the emphasizing of atmosphere and mood. Early or late lighting gives splendid opportunities for pictorial and creative colour effects.

Back-lighting too, can create a striking result, outlining subject matter with a delightful rim of light and casting dramatic shadows. It will also enhance the translucent quality of foliage and flowers and give emphasis to texture. Fountains, street scenes and yachts are all subjects which can benefit from the impact that back-lighting can give. A lens hood is a

'Evening Calm': A landscape with the ingredients of a pleasant sky, a mountain range, trees, grassland and calm water. What really brings the shot to life is the relatively small, solitary structure on the island, not only because of its position, but also the strong light of the evening sun which emphasizes it as the main point of interest.
Camera club competition award.

OM-1 Ektachrome 50mm lens 1/125th sec. @ f8.

must when you are capturing the effects of this exciting form of lighting.

Most photographers use a lens hood for back-lighting but not for other occasions. Today's lenses are coated to reduce flare but little can be done if rays of light reach the front of the lens. Unless you are seeking unusual effects by deliberately including flare, it is sensible procedure to use a lens hood when shooting brightly-lit subjects and locations with high reflectance such as swimming pools, areas of glass surfaces and the seaside.

When photographing in hazy conditions try some shots using a filter for haze penetration and also expose a few frames to accentuate a misty effect to produce an atmospheric result. Among the exciting aspects of colour is the amount of control one has in subduing or accentuating lighting conditions by using graduated filters which affect only half of the image.

When taking black-and-white pictures in strong

'Swaledale': If your primary aim is to get your photographs selected for exhibitions, it involves more than submitting pictures of good print quality. Composition, impact and appeal come high on the list of the assets required. Advice that a picture must have a principal and dominant interest does not infer that it must always be isolated with all other subject matter subdued. In this North Yorkshire scene the lighting has helped to create the mood of the picture, contrasting the zigzag walls with the open areas of grass. An elevated viewpoint was used to emphasize walls and buildings providing a number of points of interest, which are integrated in the overall arrangement.

Exhibited in the East of England Show and camera club exhibition award.

Bronica SQA   Ilford FP4   80mm lens   1/250th sec @ f8

tones are emphasized by the existing light. An example of this can be observed in the results of a scene taken in cloudy conditions and the same location photographed under a clear sky. The fundamental difference being due to the light which changed the tonal appearance.

The same tonal pattern is also evident in colour pictures, ranging perhaps from dark green foliage at one end of the scale to bright blossom at the other. In colour, the darker tones being referred to as shades and the lighter tones as tints. The wider the range of

'The Tower': Although the tower occupies a relatively small area of the picture, it has been made the focal point, with the other buildings taking a supporting role. The transparency impressed one judge because of the rendering of the tower's detail and design—made prominent by the strong light—being seen against a clear blue sky.

A camera club exhibition award winner, the picture has also been successful in inter-club competitions.

Olympus FTL   Ektachrome 64   50mm lens   1/125th sec @ f8

'Shapes and Shadows': The picture has succeeded in competitions because I was able to make the most of the lighting conditions. Photographed late in the day, the low sun caught one side of the gravestones, giving an appearance of an additional dimension. The sunlit foliage set against the church wall in shadow complemented the effect.
   Accepted for a District Arts Exhibition.

OM-1   Ektachrome 64   50mm lens   1/60th sec @ f5.6

sunlight, a reasonable assessment of the range of tones can be made by peering through half-closed eyes. By viewing a subject in this way you can visualize the overall appearance of the final result. Between the extremes of white and black lies an infinite variety of densities, each tone being affected by the diversity and strength of the light.

Tonal Range
Although variations in tonal range are always evident, in black-and-white, the contrast and luminosity of the

'Autumn Haze': Weak sunshine together with the hazy conditions of an autumn afternoon, have reduced the contrast and blurred the detail of trees, fallen leaves and the passer-by. However, the soft light and subtle colours have contributed enormously to the delicate atmosphere.
   A camera club competition prize-winner.

OM-1   Kodachrome 64   75-150mm zoom   1/60th sec @ f5.6

tones the more effective will be the representation of tone and contrast in the finished picture. Always be mindful that the light which is creating the shadows is bringing to life the tones as well.

Our assessment of mood in a picture is influenced by the tonal range reproduced and the areas of light and shade. Mood can be very apparent in a photograph of high contrast and just as powerfully evident in a picture of limited tonal range such as a misty scene of a pale background and a mid-grey foreground.

Tones and tints which are brought to life by the lighting contribute immensely to the impact and mood of a photograph. Allied to this are the lines which evolve from the overall composition. By acquiring an 'observing eye', one can be alert to take advantage of these elements and recognize the arrangement of the lines and shapes of tonal contrast.

One of the pitfalls for the newcomer to colour photography is the tendency to be impressed by areas of intense colour, another is to search for the brightest and most colourful scenes. This often results in photographs which are overpowering in colour content. Usually after the initial introduction, one acquires a better appreciation of colour and subsequently soft and subtle shades claim attention. Selective focus on a minimum area of colour set against a neutral background can rivet a judge's attention to a picture.

Methods for Colour and Black-and-White

A photographer should always be aware of the difference between shooting colour and black-and-white films. Because a subject reproduces well in colour it does not follow that a similar shot will be as successful in black-and-white and vice versa. Each medium requires a different approach. Whereas black-and-white photography comprises areas of texture, shape and contrast of tones, with colour film consideration has to be given to colour contrast as well. For instance, large patches of red and green which might be of harmonious tone in black-and-white, could cause disunity in a colour picture.

This particularly applies when using differential focus. A warm colour is just as likely to attract attention even though it might be well out of focus. In a black-and-white shot it would simply merge into the out-of-focus background but in colour photography out-of-focus colour must be treated with care. This is when a depth-of-field preview button or lever is so valuable on a camera and should always be used when considering differential focusing. The preview button is an often neglected feature in the photographer's armoury, it is only by getting into the habit of checking on the effect of larger apertures on out-of-focus areas that you will discover the varied results which can be obtained.

Warm colours such as red, orange and yellow will stand out and demand attention, but blue and green being colder will recede into a scene. Even a small area of red will attract the eye so care must be given to the positioning of a warm colour in the frame. If a picture comprised areas of red, blue and green only, red could be considered as the foremost subject matter with blue and green as the secondary colours. A photograph which contains delicate hues overall and a warm colour in a prominent position, is always extremely effective. Although many photographers work from this basis, for the adventurous and the

'Conversation': The horizontal lines of the woodwork and the white door posts provide an excellent frame for the two ladies involved in a discussion. The rich colour of the dress worn by the talker with her back to the camera demands attention because of the important position in the arrangement, but the one who really completes the picture is the smiling face of the lady in shadow.
   A camera club award winner.

OM-1   Kodachrome 64   75-150mm lens   1/125th sec @ f5.6

competition photographer it is by sometimes reversing the accepted roles of warm and cold colours that a picture becomes a prizewinner.

   A useful accessory when reverting to black-and-white photography after taking a number of colour pictures, is a monochromatic viewing filter. It enables you to view a subject or scene without being distracted by colour differences, so that you can ascertain the value of the tones which will appear as black-and-white in the final print.

Stepping Stones to Winning

When selecting an entry for a competition which does not specify a set subject, always remember that in any assessment of a large number of photographs of diverse subjects, it is sometimes the incongruous which will be the most prominent. So always be prepared to photograph something which appears to be absurd because of a certain juxtaposition of subject matter or a very ordinary object in an exceptional situation.

'Woodland': To discover that the finished print has not the picture qualities envisaged at the time the shutter release was pressed, is always disappointing. But there are occasions when an unsatisfactory result can be improved and transformed into a winner. Although 'Woodland' did convey the feeling of the scene, the lack of contrast gave the appearance of an overall dullness. Even a harder grade of printing paper did not help. It was by using the technique of contacting the original negative with lith film and eliminating all middle tones that an effective change was made. The solid black and clear white images converted the picture to a graphic representation, while maintaining the impression of the original idea.

   Exhibited at the East of England Show and Essex International Salon of Photography. Camera club trophy winner.

Original negative:
Rolleiflex T   Ilford FP4   1/125th sec @ f8

Always keep in mind the end result you are trying to accomplish and avoid being distracted or persuaded from your target. If you are taking pictures of people in silhouette against a sky background and that is the setting you intended, do not be influenced by other suggestions or attempt to change your viewpoint until you have achieved the effect you had worked out in your original plan. Once you have recorded your idea then try the alternatives. Seek to be objective and have a sense of purpose in your photography, by seeing your self-planned assignments through to a successful conclusion.

There is no special formula that will guarantee an award every time you press the shutter release, but the qualities of originality, impact, sharp detail and a pleasing range of tones are stepping stones towards producing a winning entry.

Be prepared to experiment. It is one thing to see the results of special techniques in exhibitions and magazines, but it is another matter to attempt them yourself. Whether in the basic processes or unusual methods, by participating you obtain first-hand experience, which is an essential part of a competition photographer's progress.

The more film you expose the more aware you will become of the aesthetics of composition. Basic guidelines are very useful to follow, but once understood and practised they should lead you on to cultivating and exercising your artistic senses.

By working to a set procedure you can determine at which stage an idea went wrong or quality was not maintained. If you are reasonably pleased, note which methods proved to be satisfactory. By careful deliberation in establishing the reasons for failure or success you can move towards an objective of consistent improvement and at the same time derive the maximum pleasure from your photography.

Creativity with a camera is more than just recognizing a subject which is there for the taking. It means a picture thoughtfully perceived and planned in an imaginative way. The creative photographer will seek to transform the mundane into something extraordinary by an unusual approach or by dramatic treatment.

'Windswept': Having decided to make the tree the point of interest, it was necessary to climb to a higher viewpoint so that the tree could be set against a dark background to emphasize the sunlit branches. Taken in North Wales on a bright summer's day, the fast moving clouds were continually changing the amount of light covering the distant hills and mountains which alternated between sunshine and shadow. It was a matter of waiting patiently for the tree to be bathed in sunlight with the view in the background to be covered in shadow. To give further prominence to the tree the sky was given extra exposure and darkened at the enlarging stage.

Camera club awards and exhibited at the Essex International Salon of Photography.

Kowa 66   Ilford FP4   150mm lens (orange filter)   1/250th sec @ f5.6

Processing and Printing

The moment you frame a subject in the viewfinder signals the start of a series of operations which, with reasonable care, will culminate in your original idea being presented successfully.

The Darkroom

Once you have taken your pictures the next important phase in their production is carried out in the darkroom. To develop your films and photographs is an advantage over having them processed commercially, because of the control and personal attention you can give. A slight increase in development or an improvement in composition by subtle cropping of the image when enlarging, could be the extra touch that tips the scales for success. Additionally there is the enjoyment and satisfaction derived from reproducing your own pictures.

This chapter is not a step-by-step guide to processing and darkroom operations, because there are many handbooks published for that purpose, but the subject is included to provide some pointers and methods which can increase your chances of accomplishing a competition winner.

If you do not have any darkroom facilities, do not let that deter you from entering competitions. First, make sure that the rules do not require the processing to be carried out by the photographer, then go ahead and have the work produced commercially.

When you take your films to be developed it is preferable to order a contact sheet of the negatives first, then you can select the best shots for enlargement. Remember that the size of enlargement will partly depend on the quality of the negative and the area to be used. If the negative is unsharp the fault will become more noticeable as the size of the picture is increased.

If you are able to set aside a spare room as a darkroom, it does save time in unpacking and setting up your equipment before every processing session. However, it is surprising what can be achieved by improvising and making use of the bathroom or kitchen, provided the windows and gaps around the doors can be effectively blacked out. Fresh air is important, with special attention given to keeping water away from electrical wiring and ensuring all plugs and sockets are correctly earthed.

To have running water and a sink in your darkroom is convenient but not essential. After films or prints are fixed they can be immersed in a bucket of water and then taken to another room for final washing. Practically any room in a house can be utilized as a temporary darkroom provided that it is not too dusty and there is some form of ventilation.

Very little equipment is required to develop films

'Church Porch': Photographers interested in architecture are often advised to first take a picture of the complete building and then to look around the structure to find more effective viewpoints. My reason for photographing this part of the church was that the late afternoon sun had accentuated the style of the porch and brought out the texture of the stonework epitomizing the building's character. Although some detail is apparent inside the entrance, the area of shadow has not been lightened further as the dark tone strengthens the remainder of the picture.
Exhibited at the Essex International Salon of Photography.

Rolleiflex T   Ilford FP4   75mm lens   1/125th sec @ f11

and make contact prints for preliminary viewing and selection. By using a changing bag the exposed film can be inserted into a developing tank without the need to black out the room. Once the film has been loaded on to the spiral and the lid closed, processing can be carried out in daylight.

'Cul-de-sac': One of the reasons which prompted me to submit this photograph to exhibitions was the wide range of tones, brought about by the delightful back-lighting. Without the strong light, the picture would have appeared to be overcrowded with detail and with no prominent point of interest. The angle of light has given a strong outline and separation of the lamps, stonework and window-box plants. Another contributing factor to the success of the picture is the strong reflectance value of the walls which has lightened the shadow areas.

Exhibited at the Essex International Salon of Photography and the East of England Show.

Rolleiflex T   Ilford FP4   75mm
lens   1/250th sec @ f11

The Ideal Negative

The excellence of the finished print is dependent on a number of factors and most certainly upon the qualities of a good negative. The ideal negative, that is, one which has been correctly exposed and developed, will contain a good range of tones with detail in the shadows and adequate density in the highlights—and will be suitable for printing on to a normal grade of paper.

One way of determining whether a black-and-white negative has been correctly exposed and developed is to place it emulsion side down over a printed page of a book. The type matter should be just about readable through the densest highlight, while shadow detail should be perceptible in the thinnest areas of the film. Some negatives will fall short of the quality required by being too contrasty and others will be too flat. For these it will be necessary to match the negative to a specific grade of paper. As an average guide, negatives of very high contrast require soft grade paper, whereas negatives which are too flat need a hard grade.

Blemish-free negatives are very important, so all solutions should be carefully filtered and development carried out by the time and temperature method. It is also beneficial to add a few drops of wetting agent to the water in the tank at the conclusion of the final wash to promote even drying. As a further safeguard against marks and imperfections try to avoid cleaning your darkroom immediately before processing a film or a printing session.

Developing colour negative film takes longer than processing black-and-white negatives, it is not difficult but does require precise timing and accurate control in keeping the developer at the correct temperature. You cannot evaluate the quality of colour negatives in the same way as with black-and-white film because the dye images are not so easy to assess.

Reversal Films

Most colour reversal film can be home-processed, but there is not a great advantage in this unless you wish to see the results without delay. Precise processing is a must as the best results are obtained by keeping strictly to the manufacturer's recommendations.

Some colour reversal films can have the effective film speed increased by extending the time of the film in the first developer. By this technique a film rated at ISO 400/27° could be exposed at ISO 800/30° or more, quite successfully. The more a film is 'pushed' in this way so the grain will become coarser and contrast will be increased. Whenever a film is uprated remember that every frame must be exposed at the higher rating. Certain laboratories undertake to modify development for up or down rating at a reasonable extra cost. It is absolutely essential that any film which has been rated differently should be clearly marked with your special instructions.

It is always tempting to experiment with various film and developer combinations. There are some black-and-white film developers which give a useful film speed increase whereas others have the effect of reducing the speed rating but give an improvement in fine grain. Some show both a speed increase and an apparent enhancement in sharpness. Although trying out films and developers can be very absorbing, try to become completely familiar with one type of film and chemicals before considering other alternatives.

'Breaking Through': Interesting and unusual pictures are often possible before or after a storm. Bad weather photography is not to everyone's liking, but thunderclouds can provide a dramatic element to a landscape or seascape picture. Generally, it is the moments after a storm when the clouds begin to move away that the shafts of light break through to make a dramatic impression. There was little time to try another viewpoint but exposure was kept to a minimum to give full emphasis to the sky.
   Camera club award.

OM-1   Kodachrome 64   75-150mm zoom   1/60th sec @ f5.6

Contact Prints

Once you have developed your film it is essential to view the images in positive form before subsequent enlargement. This is when a contact sheet of the whole film can be a significant stage in the production of a competition print. Contact printing frames are specially manufactured for this purpose. A 35mm model will take a 36 exposure film, divided into six strips of six exposures. A frame for negative size 6 x 6 cm will accept a 120 size film divided into four strips of three negatives.

Every contact sheet should receive the same care that you would give to an enlargement. By standardising your processing you will be able to consistently produce good quality results which will enable you to assess the potential of the negative and the likely format of the ensuing enlargement.

An inexpensive method of reproducing the detail of colour negatives for viewing in positive form is to print a contact sheet from them in black and white. This is quite adequate for preliminary assessment, but for further consideration a full colour contact sheet is the only answer.

If your output does not justify investing in a contact poof printer, contact prints can be obtained by placing a bromide sheet of paper, face side up and positioning the negatives emulsion side down. A piece of clean plate-glass, large enough to cover the negatives should be used to keep the film flat and in good contact with the paper while being exposed.

This routine is satisfactory when working under normal safelight conditions for black-and-white printing, but with full colour contact prints it is necessary to work in complete darkness. To make it easier to handle the negatives, fix the colour film to the glass with masking tape with the emulsion side of the negative away from the glass surface. This can be done in ordinary room light or safelight conditions. After the negatives are positioned, the light is switched off and the negatives are placed in contact with the printing paper for exposure.

When the contact sheets have been processed they can be examined at leisure with a magnifying glass. Areas selected for enlargement can be indicated with a chinagraph pencil. When choosing negatives for enlargement, remember that the finished print does not have to conform to the shape of the negative. A useful aid when assessing your work is to use two L-shaped pieces of card. By laying them over the picture area in various positions one is able to change the shape and appearance of the print until the most pleasing arrangement is achieved. On occasions when you are undecided about composition, it can be helpful to turn the print upside down. This method sometimes reveals unbalanced masses of tone and areas of competing interest which have been overlooked.

Enlargers

An enlarger is a vital item of equipment in the darkroom and should be of strong construction and remain rigid and free from vibration while the paper is being exposed. All the controls and levers should be easily accessible, and the focusing mechanism working smoothly to enable fine focusing of the

'Antique Shop': The old Essex town of Thaxted was once a flourishing wool and cloth centre. These days the wonderfully preserved half-timbered and plastered buildings attract much interest from visitors to the area. While taking some shots in the town I noticed the two youngsters waiting patiently and included them in the composition. Although prominent, they do not become over important because of the fascinating shapes and tones of the architecture.

Exhibited at the Essex International Salon of Photography, also a camera club exhibition award winner.

Rolleiflex T   Ilford FP4   75mm lens   1/250th sec @ f5.6

projected image. The lens too, should be of good quality, and the best you can afford, for there is little point in producing pin-sharp, well-exposed negatives if the end product is to be spoiled by an inferior enlarging lens.

The lamp illumination should be evenly distributed over the whole picture area and the enlarger should be placed on a firm support which will remain perfectly steady while exposures are made. If your enlarger does not have the feature of automatic focusing, a worthwhile darkroom accessory is a focus finder. With this you actually focus on the grain of the negative to ensure a sharp result.

Most enlargers manufactured these days are made

for colour or can be adapted. Enlargers to be used for making colour prints require either a drawer for inserting filters between the light source and the negative, or a colour head that incorporates the filters which are operated by a set of coded dials.

Voltage fluctuation can affect the intensity of the enlarger illumination and also the colour quality, so if your colour printing output is on a large scale, a constant voltage stabilizer can be a worthwhile investment.

Check that the safelight is really safe and that the bulb is the correct wattage. Always ensure that the developer and fixer are fresh and that the dishes are not contaminated with other chemicals. In the continual quest for quality, always clean both sides of a negative with a soft dusting brush before inserting it into the enlarger carrier, which should hold the negative perfectly flat. Do not brush too vigorously otherwise you will charge the surface with static electricity and attract more dust than you brush away.

Test Strips

Making a test strip before producing an enlargement is a method of obtaining the correct exposure and keeping the amount of wasted printing paper to a minimum.

First check that the image on the baseboard is in sharp focus and the lens stopped down. Then cut a strip of paper from a sheet of the same packet which you intend to use for the enlargement. Place the unexposed paper on an area of the image which is representative of the remainder of the negative. Then with a piece of opaque card, which is larger than the test strip, shield the paper, switch on the enlarger lamp and expose the paper in a series of steps by moving the card across the paper every five seconds. This will give a strip of four different exposures of 5, 10, 15 and 20 seconds. It is essential that the test-strip receives careful development and that the exposure given to the portion subsequently chosen is repeated for the enlargement.

If the test strip shows all the steps as too dark, try another with less exposure or close the lens aperture by one stop. Conversely if the strips are too light, increase the exposure accordingly or open the lens aperture. Never make a decision on which exposure to select for enlarging by viewing the strip by safelight. Always switch the main light on for a precise evaluation.

Black-and-White Printing Papers

For most black-and-white competitions white glossy paper is ideal, especially for its qualities in reproducing very fine detail and its maximum brightness range, making it a good choice for the majority of subjects. There are occasions when other papers can also be used advantageously; in addition to white, papers with a tinted base can be obtained. Whereas a white base contributes to brilliant highlights and rich natural blacks, tinted bases produce a much warmer effect which suits portraits and some pictorial subjects.

There is a choice of paper surfaces which, in addition to glossy, includes lustre, pearl, satin, stipple, semi-matt and matt. Although fine lustre does not possess the brilliance of glossy paper, it has a slight sheen which enhances pictorial subjects. Semi-matt has a very fine texture and is suitable for pictures which require a soft delicate appearance. It is also an excellent base for pencil retouching. The ranges of tint and texture surfaces are used widely for exhibitions and photographic club competitions, but they can be used effectively for some subjects in open contests. No paper surface is ideal for every type of subject matter; very often the choice is made according to personal preference. In many instances it will be found that manufacturers give their own descriptions to the various surfaces.

The advantages of single-weight enlarging paper, apart from being easier to glaze, are that it is less expensive, and if you are sending a number of prints in the same envelope, cheaper to post. For lustre and unglazed surfaces, double-weight paper is preferable, especially for large prints which are to be mounted.

Resin-coated papers are convenient for reproducing a finished print in the quickest time (made possible by a washing time of about four minutes), whereas the recommended washing time for fibre-based double weight paper is 45 minutes. Although resin-coated papers are not advised for archival purposes they are excellent if you are in a hurry and trying to meet a competition deadline.

Nearly all black-and-white papers are compatible with the many print developers, the most noticeable difference being in the image colour when warm-toned developers are used.

Shading and Burning-In

Good darkroom technique can impart the requisite quality which is necessary to make a print a winner. Varying the exposure for different areas of a photograph during enlarging can improve a washed-out or dense appearance. For general areas which require less exposure, shading can be achieved by using your hand or a piece of card between the lens and the baseboard. By employing your hand and fingers to form shapes it is possible to shield specific portions from the enlarging lamp while giving the remainder of the print the required exposure.

Dodging is similar to shading except that it is suitable for smaller areas and is carried out by attaching a piece of black card to a thin piece of wire so that you can give a small area less exposure without affecting the whole photograph. Black card is preferable to a light colour as it prevents light being

bounced back to the printing paper.

Burning-in is applied after giving the main exposure by using a piece of card with a hole cut out of the middle. Extra exposure can then be given to the area requiring more detail. Whichever form is used keep your hand or piece of card well above the printing paper on the baseboard and keep the card moving throughout the additional exposure time so that no hard edges appear on the print.

Water-Bath Development

There are occasions when even careful shading cannot prevent shadow areas of prints darkening to the extent that all detail is lost. It is sometimes possible to retrieve the situation by using the technique of water-bath development, which holds back developer activity in the shadow areas while allowing the highlights to continue to develop.

Immediately the first images of development appear lift the print from the developer and immerse in a dish of water and still-bath for about one minute. Then return the print to the developer. As soon as the image begins to darken, transfer the print to the water bath

'Road Works': A lens-hood was essential for this against-the-light shot. The elevated viewpoint has given depth to the picture, separating the workman in a way which would not have been possible at ground level. The higher camera position has also shown the smoke and steam to good effect which has contributed to the display of a good range of tones.

This photograph has had success in exhibitions including the Essex Salon and also a camera club exhibition award.

Rolleiflex T   Ilford FP3   75mm lens   1/125th sec @ f5.6

as before. The procedure is continued until a satisfactory image is obtained, then the print is fixed in the usual way.

The effect of this method is that while the developer is retained in the emulsion, development continues when the print is still-bathed in water. The developer's activity is soon exhausted in the shadow areas but its action continues for a lot longer in the highlights where there is less image. The routine is useful for reducing contrast and bringing out detail in skies where other subject matter such as tree branches prevent any dodging techniques. It is also a

91

Opposite page: '**Towards Kettlewell**': The shot was taken in the beautiful Wharfedale area of North Yorkshire on a sunny day in late October. In addition to the choice of viewpoint and the positioning of the hiker, the success of this kind of atmosphere picture often depends on specific work in the darkroom. Attention was given to dodging and shading particular areas at the enlarging stage to give emphasis to the path and woodwork of the bridge. Selective exposure was also given to the middle distance to maintain detail and the hazy appearance.

Winner of the Bedford Perpetual Challenge Trophy and a £50 award for being adjudged the best print in the East of England Show Open Exhibition. The picture received a further prize of £10 presented by The Royal Photographic Society for the best print exhibited by an RPS member. The judgement criterion was that the print should show outstanding or unusual treatment of its subject matter.

Bronica SOA   Ilford FP4   80mm lens   1/125th sec @ f5.6

Below: '**Dale Farm**': I would have preferred to have been able to include more open space on each side of the picture. Unfortunately the scene required tight framing to eliminate details which would have been distracting and would have marred the presentation of an uncomplicated design. With the largest shed in a dominant position the remainder of the picture is balanced by the smaller sheds and fence.

A camera club exhibition award winner.

OM-1   Kodachrome 64   75-150mm zoom   1/125th sec @ f5.6

means of balancing contrast in pictures which include exterior and interior light sources.

Colour Printing Papers

Colour printing paper is extremely sensitive to nearly all parts of the visible spectrum. A very dim yellow-green safelight can be used when working with colour paper in the darkroom, but only for the purpose of identifying objects and equipment. If there is the slightest chance of fogging the paper it is preferable to do without a safelight altogether.

Colour prints can be developed in a dish or in a print processing drum which is far more convenient for home colour-processing. The system is economical as the drum requires a minimum quantity of chemicals for each process. By using fresh chemicals for each print, consistent print quality can be maintained. Apart from inserting the exposed printing paper into the drum, all the processing stages can be carried out in normal room lighting.

For the photographer who wishes to enter contests which require colour prints, but only shoots colour reversal film, the answer is to enlarge the transparencies on to colour reversal paper. One of the advantages of making colour prints by this method is that the transparency and the projected positive

'Columns': The problem of converging verticals in this picture was corrected when making the enlargement, by tilting the masking frame. The photograph shows part of the National Gallery of Art in Washington D.C. After the composition was decided upon, the exposure was delayed until someone walked up the steps and reached an appropriate position. One change from the original scene is that the negative has been reversed from left to right in order to improve the composition and allow the handrail to be positioned from the bottom left taking the viewer up and to the right of the picture. This is quite permissible unless you are claiming the picture is an exact record.

Exhibited East of England Show and winner of the premier print trophy in the Basildon District Arts Association's Rosebowl awards for photography.

Rolleiflex T   Ilford FP4   75mm lens   1/125th sec @ f11

image is a guide to what the finished result should be.

The best transparencies for reproduction as colour prints are those which are not too contrasty and display good colour saturation, therefore a slightly under-exposed slide is preferable to one which is over-exposed.

When enlarging colour transparencies on to reversal printing paper you will be able to use the techniques of burning-in and shading in a similar way as with black-and-white printing. The extra attention is worthwhile and necessary to achieving optimum quality.

Reversal paper is produced in one grade only, it is of low contrast and therefore ideal for transparencies which are usually more contrasty than negatives. On the occasions when contrast is excessive, one way of easing it is to resort to flashing. First expose the printing paper in the normal way with the transparency and filter in place, then remove the transparency

and give a brief flashing exposure which will bring up the middle tones.

Always keep a note of the filtration and exposure for any colour print for future reference.

Converging Verticals

Although it is preferable to avoid converging verticals when taking the photograph, there are situations when the camera has to be tilted to include a high point of a building. When this has occurred it is feasible to make some correction at the printing session by raising one end of the masking frame on the enlarger baseboard, and supporting it with a book or something similar in size. After you have tilted the masking frame sufficiently to eliminate any convergence, carefully focus the image and stop the lens well down to maintain sharpness over the entire print. The raised end of the printing paper will be nearer the enlarging lens so it will receive more exposure than the remainder of the sheet. Therefore, it will be necessary to progressively increase the exposure over the rest of the print in order to obtain an evenly reproduced image. On some enlargers both the film and lens planes can be tilted to maintain full image sharpness. If the film carrier and masking frame can both be tilted in opposite directions, the angle to which each is tilted is reduced and gives better distortion control.

The Right Picture Size

Whenever possible submit photographs of 10″ x 8″ (25.4 x 20.3 cm) size. Although size alone is not enough to win a competition, the comparison of an enprint with a 10″ x 8″ enlargement will illustrate the advantage of the larger size. The bigger area will reveal detail and tonal quality which will not be apparent in enprint and small contact-print sizes. Unless requested in the contest rules it is not advisable to submit any photograph smaller than 7″ x 5″ (17.8 x 12.7 cm).

Filing Negatives

A matter not to be overlooked when submitting an entry is the safe keeping of the negatives. One should adopt a simple filing system and store the negatives in translucent envelopes for protection against dust. For convenience, 35mm size negatives can be filed in strips of five frames for a 20-exposure film and a 36-exposure length can be cut into strips of six. Larger films such as 120 size can also be cut into strips or if preferred, each negative can be filed individually. It should be noted that some processing laboratories do not undertake printing from single negatives which have been cut from a length of film.

Negative filing sheets can be purchased in various sizes. Each sheet is made to fit into a ring binder, and has sleeves to accommodate the cut strips of a complete film. The system you employ must be suitable for expansion and all negatives easy to locate. Beware of cellophane envelopes as they can be affected by moisture and ensure that your negative files are stored in a clean and dry place.

An uncomplicated method of keeping a visual record of your negatives is to contact print a complete film on to a 10″ x 8″ (25.4 x 20.3 cm) sheet of printing paper. The negative numbers which appear on the film edge are also reproduced on the contact print and are useful for identification purposes and can be incorporated in the indexing system you use.

'Annual Event': When I set about producing a shot illustrating the conker season I decided to feature the conkers rather than the facial expressions of the conker players. Care was taken to keep the background out of focus to give maximum prominence to the conkers and string. From a number of exposures that were made, this shot was the best representation of the arrangement I was attempting to achieve.

The print received a highly commended award at the East of England Show Photographic Exhibition.

Rolleiflex T   Ilford FP4   75mm lens   1/250th sec @ f4

Presentation

Always judge your competition entries yourself before despatching them. No matter how pleasing the subject and composition may be, you can still lose points because of a poorly finished enlargement. Eliminate any photograph that is not sharp or which is badly printed. If the contest rules permit an unlimited number of prints, refrain from sending anything below standard. It is preferable to enter one good print than to submit a number of mediocre pictures.

Judge for Yourself

The observations of knowledgeable friends can be helpful too as they can comment as viewers only, whereas the photographer must always exclude any influencing thoughts of difficulties overcome or pleasant memories of the circumstances which existed when the picture was taken. Judges of course, are impressed only by what is placed before them. Therefore, any pre-judging of one's work which is attempted personally, should be done as dispassionately as possible.

Eliminate Blemishes

Take care in examining your prints for defects. Entries which succeed in reaching the final stages of a contest will be viewed closely, so it is important that white spots and other blemishes which may appear on a finished photograph should be spotted out with a dye or spotting medium. The offending marks are usually attributable to dust which settles on the film during drying or at the enlarging stage. Obviously blemishes are more conspicuous at the bigger degrees of enlargement. Sometimes it will not be a processing fault but a small highlight area which you may wish to darken because it draws attention away from more important parts of the picture.

Glossy retouching water colour paint, which can be purchased in small tubes, is ideal for spotting out dust marks and hair lines and is suitable for all kinds of printing papers except matt surfaces which tend to emphasize any glossy retouching on larger areas. The blue-black paint is mixed with water to the desired shade and applied with the very fine point of a good quality artist's brush size 2 or 3. The spotting medium does not dry out so rapidly with these sizes as with the extremely small brushes. Always buy best quality sable brushes and ensure they are cleaned thoroughly after use. Retouching outfits are available if you prefer to purchase a complete kit.

If you have not attempted retouching before, it is recommended that you experiment on an unwanted print first. Work with the brush almost dry, moistening it first with water, then retouching pigment. Wipe the

'Mosque in Acre': If I had tilted the camera to include the whole of the mosque, the result would have shown converging verticals. One alternative, which I followed, was to concentrate attention on the delightful soft colours and include more foreground which fortunately displayed detail in the form of paving stones and shadows.
Camera club competition award.

Olympus FTL   Ektachrome 64   50mm lens   1/125th sec @ f5.6

brush on white paper to remove surplus pigment and at the same time assess the strength of colour which is to match the area surrounding the blemish. Keep the brush almost vertical and make a succession of minute dots until the blemish conforms to the tone of the adjacent area.

Prints that are produced on matt or lustre surface

papers can be retouched with a soft grade lead pencil, preferably HB. Sharpen the lead to a very fine point for spotting, and hold the pencil almost upright, ensuring that undue pressure on the print is avoided. An advantage of retouching with a pencil is that any marks made in error are easily rubbed off with a soft cloth. Pencil work is unsuitable for glossy paper.

Large white spots require a lot of patience. Never try to fill the whole area with a few strokes of the brush, but apply the pigment unhurriedly with fine stippling. Work around the edge of the blemish with the brush held vertically, wait for the pigment to dry then continue spotting, gradually moving towards the middle of the blemish until the area is filled. Great care is needed in keeping the brush as dry as possible otherwise you are likely to lift off adjacent stippling. White hair lines can be disguised in a similar way, being filled in with a series of small spots instead of attempting to fill in the lines with a continuous sweep of the brush. An advantage of using water colour is that any error can be removed by dabbing with a moistened cloth. Allow the surface to dry before starting again.

High Gloss Finish

When working on prints which have a glossy surface,

'Lakeland': The day I took this shot had been disappointing photographically, with only a few breaks in the cloud. Having driven to this area of the Lake District I admired the scene through the viewfinder: a pleasing arrangement, which led the eye to and from the tree. Human interest was required. Strollers made their way to the water and back without improving the composition, that is until the two figures dressed in bright clothing came along and the sun filtered through to complete the picture.
Camera club competition award.

OM-1   Kodachrome 64   75-150mm zoom   1/125th sec @ f5.6

you can impart a sheen on the retouched area, by stroking the brush on gummed paper—the flap of an envelope will do—each time the brush is re-moistened with water colour.

Black spots are not so common but are more difficult to remove. They can be deleted by knifework, which involves scraping away the surface of the emulsion very lightly with a retouching knife. A useful tool for print retouching is a scalpel holder which can be used with blades of various shapes. It is important to always work with a sharp blade. The result of each knife stroke should be almost imperceptible, otherwise it is possible to penetrate the emulsion and make the blemish far worse. It is also essential that the print is completely dry. It must be emphasized that any knifework requires considerable skill and together with other retouching methods is something to be learned by experience and patience.

An alternative method is to bleach the black marks with a photographic chemical reducer, a solution of hypo and potassium ferricyanide. Minute applications of the reducer are applied to the surface of the print with a fine brush until the blemishes are removed. The print is then thoroughly washed and when dry the bleached areas are retouched as previously described.

The retouching of black spots on a colour print is more difficult, any attempt at knifing with a scalpel blade means scraping through three layers of colour. So rather than bleaching or scraping it is safer to disguise offending marks by using retouching colours. Another method of overcoming a black mark on a colour print is to fill in the blemish on the negative and then retouch the subsequent white area on the print. For white spots, colour retouching dye should be used; if the spots are very small it is possible to touch them in with diluted black water colour.

Retouching can be made easier and the finished result more satisfactory with the aid of a quality magnifier and a good light to ensure the photograph is well illuminated. No matter how skilled you become it is worth remembering the adage that prevention is better than cure. For those who do their own processing, the time spent filtering solutions and eliminating dust at the enlarging stage will be a decisive factor in restricting defects to a minimum.

White glossy paper has already been referred to as being ideal for competition entries, because of the full range of tones and detail it can reproduce. There are two types of black-and-white paper available—resin-coated and fibre-based. Apart from the advantages of rapid processing, resin-coated glossy paper dries naturally to a superb high gloss finish.

With the popularity of resin-coated papers, glazing is a process that is not used much these days. However, fibre-based glossy paper can either be glazed to a mirror-like finish or left unglazed. If the former, ensure that the glazed surface is free from patchiness. A competition entry that is unglazed is unquestionably preferable to one which has been poorly glazed.

An electrically heated print dryer-glazer plus a good quality glazing plate are a worthwhile investment if you intend to do a lot of glazing with fibre-based paper. Always maintain the glazing plate in perfect condition by keeping it free from scratches and well protected when not in use.

Careful attention to glazing procedure is essential if a high gloss finish is to be achieved. Make sure the prints are fully fixed and thoroughly washed in clean water. Imperfections in a glazed surface can be caused by impurities in the water supply and this can be obviated by fitting a filter to the tap. After washing, place the print on the glazing plate and press the surfaces into close contact with a squeegee, expelling surplus water and any trapped air bubbles. An important point is to ensure that the cloth cover of the dryer is tensioned sufficiently to retain the print and plate firmly together until the print springs from the plate when glazed and dry.

Although there are not many manufacturers who produce single-weight paper these days, it will be found that fibre-based single-weight paper is easier to glaze than double-weight.

Trimming

Whether a photograph is trimmed to leave a white border or trimmed to bleed on all sides is a matter of personal preference. Whatever style is used, an accurate cut and clean edges are imperative for presentation. All trimming should be carefully carried out with a hand guillotine or a trimming knife used with a straight-edge or steel ruler.

Mounting

Competitions which are sponsored by magazines and the press seldom require prints to be mounted, but it is usually a condition for club competitions and exhibitions. Extra thick cardboard mounts are marketed in various sizes and are available in a number of colours. Always purchase good quality mounting boards which have been specially made for photographic use, otherwise you can run the risk of any impurities in the board affecting the print over a period of time.

Black-and-white prints are often seen on white mounts but they can also be very effectively displayed on black or grey boards. The mounting of colour prints is an entirely different matter. A colour photograph placed on white can easily lose some of its colour appeal, but if mounted on brown or grey, for example, the richness of colour will be accentuated. Do be wary of brightly coloured mounts which can vie for attention and even overpower delicate pastel shades and tones of a photograph.

When you do require to mount your prints remember that it is an important aspect of showing your photographs in the most effective way. Although styles of mounting change from time to time, of the several ways of presenting a print there is no one method which can be asserted as being superior. The criterion is which style is going to enhance the print most. Flush mounting is always a way out of the problem if you are undecided about the kind of mount to use.

A disadvantage of flush mounting is that when the corners suffer any damage, the only way that it can be rectified is by re-trimming the print, whereas when a photograph is mounted with a border, any damage to the corners entails the mount only to be re-trimmed with the print area remaining untouched.

Another kind of presentation which helps to preserve the corners of photographs from being damaged is to use two mounting boards. After mounting the print by your usual method take another board and cut out a rectangular aperture or the shape required and then secure the windowed overmat to the mounted print. The important factor is to achieve the best presentation of your picture, not with a mount that will distract the viewer or overpower the subject matter, but one that will enhance the picture.

When positioning a print on the mount the conventional method of equal margins at the top and each side, with a wider margin at the base is quite satisfactory for the majority of pictures. A photograph centred exactly with equal margins at the top and bottom rarely appears to be optically correct so always include additional space at the base.

There are a number of mounting adhesives to choose from, among those widely used are the following:

Dry Mounting Tissue: A sheet of tissue, impregnated with shellac is placed between the print and mount and melted by the application of heat. This can be done by using a heated mounting press or a domestic iron used at the silk setting. The tissue should be attached to the back of the print by tacking it with the tip of a hot iron. The print and tissue are trimmed together, then placed on the mount and covered with a clean cloth and lightly ironed over the whole area. With this method the correct temperature is essential so that the tissue adheres to the print and mount simultaneously. If the iron is too hot, the tissue will stick to the mount but not to the print; if the iron is too cool, the tissue will stick to the print only. Resin-coated papers can easily be ruined by this process as the resin content of the paper can melt as quickly as the dry mounting tissue. Special mounting tissues which melt at low temperatures are obtainable for resin-coated papers.

Rubber Solution: The mount and the reverse side of the print are coated with a very thin layer of solution and brought together for adhesion when almost dry. The print is then rubbed down on to the mount. An advantage of using rubber solution is that any surplus solution can be rubbed off the surface of the print or mount. It is important to use only rubber solution which is manufactured specifically for photographic use.

Print Mountant: The mountant is painted on to the reverse side of the print only, and when dry, the print is ironed on to the mount with pressure from a hot iron.

Spray Mountant: A simple method of bonding the print to the mount is to coat the back of the print and the mount with aerosol spray adhesive, and when tacky, press both surfaces together and apply pressure to ensure good contact.

Double-sided Adhesive Tape: The tape is first affixed to the back of the untrimmed print, after which

'Tree and Shadow': Looking down from a high vantage point revealed an unfamiliar view of the tree and its shadow merging in a continuous curved line. The additional human interest would have completed a very satisfactory composition provided the couple had been seated nearer to the right of the picture. On such occasions the photographer is advised to move the camera's viewpoint to improve the picture arrangement. Unfortunately my parapet position made any move out of the question so the composition remained unchanged. Camera club competition award.

OM-1 Kodachrome 64 75-150mm zoom (85c filter) 1/125th sec @ f5.6

the print and tape are trimmed. The protective paper is then peeled from the double-sided tape which enables the print to be placed on the mount and pressed down in position.

Both spray mountant and double-sided tape are ideal for mounting plastic-base and resin-coated papers.

Making a Good Impression

Attention to presentation is just as vital when submitting photographs to a contest which requires an entry of more than one print. A group of three good pictures will convey a far better impression than an unbalanced set of one outstanding picture and two shots of a lower quality. In a similar way, whether you submit a set of prints with a white border or trim them flush, ensure that your method of presentation is identical for each picture. Avoid sending a set of prints of different sizes. The standard should be that in any set submitted, the photographs should complement each other.

The same considerations apply when a portfolio of prints or transparencies is being submitted perhaps for a 'Photographer of the Month' award or a comparable magazine competition. Once again different sizes or various paper surfaces suggest a haphazard approach, whereas a well produced portfolio which displays conformity in presentation will indicate that the photographer has a personal style and also increase the appeal of the pictures.

Prints that have areas of light tone near the edge can benefit from black borders. An uncomplicated way of achieving black borders is to expose the edges of the printing paper to the enlarger lamp before or after you have printed the image. This can be done by covering the remainder of the paper and exposing one edge at a time to the light.

Titles

It has been said that a title is superfluous because a picture should say it all. In certain cases this is true, but there are also subjects, in a humorous category for example, where a title can sustain the theme. Titles are normally requested for exhibition entries and are desirable for catalogue purposes.

When a title is required, do avoid an elaborate caption when one or two words would be just as effective. Refrain from using anything that sounds flowery. Do not try to make a print suitable for a certain category by giving it an exaggerated descrip-

'Way-out People': While taking photographs in an Air and Space Museum I was attracted by the distorted images in the highly reflective surface. The juxtaposition of an exit sign and the reflection of people walking down a gangway, prompted the title of the picture.
    Award winner in a camera club competition.

OM-1   Kodachrome 64   50mm lens   1/60th sec @ f5.6.

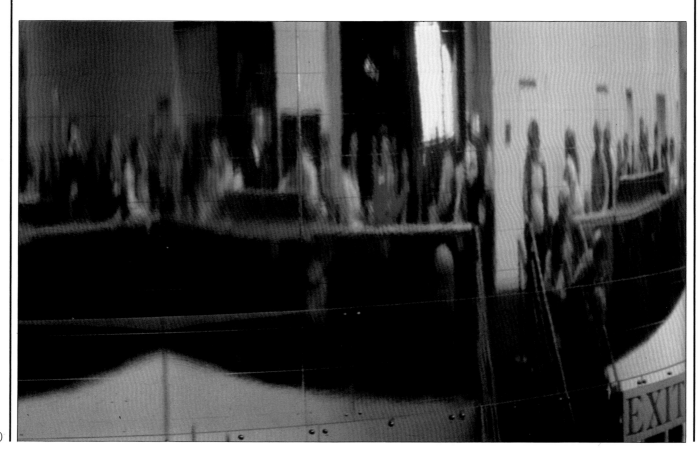

tion. A photograph entitled 'Summer Stroll' will not sway the opinion of the judges at all, if the subject reveals that 'Winter Walk' would be more accurate.

A pertinent title will not be detrimental to a good picture, so careful consideration should always be given to choosing a title that will be complementary to the subject matter.

Packing and Mailing Prints

To ensure that your photographs arrive in immaculate condition send them in a card-backed envelope or insert a sheet of rigid cardboard into a good quality envelope. In a competition where thousands of prints are entered it is possible that the stiffener will be separated or lost, and your photograph returned with a piece of cardboard too small for suitable protection or, worse still, no card returned at all.

One way of overcoming the problem is to send your photograph in an envelope which is just large enough for the return envelope to be included without being folded, and insert a cardboard stiffener into the return envelope. By inserting the stiffener yourself you make less work in the organizer's office and also ensure that your photograph will be satisfactorily protected on its return journey. An important point is to make sure that the stiffener is extra-strong cardboard, as anything less than rigid will inevitably result in cracked and spoiled photographs, unfit for further presentation. As an additional safeguard, write the words 'Photographs—please do not bend' on the front and back of each envelope.

Remember to write your name and address and also affix the correct value of postage stamps on the return envelope. If you enter a competition promoted from another country, instead of affixing stamps on the envelope it will be necessary to purchase International Reply Coupons from the post office and send the coupons with your entry for the return postage. The overseas organizers will then exchange the coupons for stamps at their post office for the return mailing.

Always use good quality envelopes. If you consider it necessary to reinforce the gummed flap with adhesive tape restrict the extra sealing to one strip only. An envelope which has been over-bound with tape for protection is difficult to open and therefore increases the chances of damage to the prints when they are eventually being extracted.

Before finally sealing the envelope ensure that your name and address are clearly written on the reverse of the photograph, also the title and other details which are required by the competition rules. Anything written on the reverse side of a print should be done with extreme care as undue pressure from a pen or pencil can cause obtrusive marks on the face-side. A felt tipped pen is most useful and will enable you to write without any impression showing on the print surface.

'Ancient Arches': The repetition of the arches was the interesting aspect that I wanted to record, which meant obtaining a viewpoint that maintained their connection, yet provided separation of the individual curves. The sandy ground proved to be a good reflector, showing detail and texture in the shadows. The satisfactory conclusion of the picture is the detail visible through the arches, including someone walking down the steps.
  Camera club competition award.

Olympus FTL   Ektachrome 64   50mm lens   1/125th sec @ f8

An alternative method is to write all the details on a piece of paper approximately half the size of the print and affix the top edge to the back of the print with a strip of clear adhesive tape. As a precaution against the unlikely happening of the details being separated, your name should be lightly written on the reverse of the print as well. If an entry form has to be included, this too can be attached as described.

Editors of photographic publications usually require the following technical data to be sent with

'Aysgarth': The advice that the part can be more successful than the whole certainly applies to waterfalls. It is often recommended that anyone photographing a waterfall should resist any impulse to include the whole scene. An overall view does lessen the impact of the flowing water but there is a place for both approaches. The shot of Aysgarth portrays a reasonable area of the falls, with the foliage providing colour, framing, and another dimension to the picture.
Camera club award winner.

OM-1 Kodachrome 64 75-150mm zoom 1/125th sec @ f8

competition entries: make of camera, focal length of lens, aperture and shutter speed, type of film and developer used.

When sending more than one entry to a popular competition it is worth considering mailing the prints individually. The advantage of this is that your work will probably be seen separately and at different times, whereas prints sent in one batch are likely to be viewed and judged side by side. Another benefit of sending prints singly is that it helps to forestall the non-arrival of your entire entry, should the envelope be delayed or lost in the post. When the rules do not restrict the number of entries, always remember that it is quality, not quantity that will win the honours.

Packing and Mailing Transparencies

Transparencies too, require systematic attention before being submitted. It is essential that they are adequately packed and protected against damage. This applies whether they are sent in cardboard or plastic mounts.

If the transparency is mounted in a plastic and glass mount ensure that the glass and transparency are absolutely clean, as any dust will be shown as unsightly blemishes when projected on to a screen. An anti-static cloth is ideal for cleaning the glass and frames, and a soft-haired brush will be useful for removing dust from the transparency.

Carefully check the rules of entry as many competitions do not accept transparencies mounted in glass. Should the glass be broken or splintered in transit, the danger is two-fold: firstly to the person who opens the package, and secondly, the splintered glass invariably damages the transparency.

If you send your entry in a cardboard mount ensure that your name, address, title of slide and any other details required, are clearly written on the mount. For plastic mounts it is preferable to write your name and address on a self-adhesive label which can be firmly affixed to the mount. Gummed paper is unsuitable as it is easily dislodged. With card or plastic glassless mounts, a transparency is always vulnerable to fingermarks, dust and scratches. The best method for protecting the film is to put the mounted transparency into a transparent sleeve or envelope. The slide can then be viewed easily without being removed from the sleeve.

Make sure that the mount is correctly spotted (marked) so that when the slide is projected the picture will appear the way you intended. For correct viewing on the screen, hold the transparency the way it should appear, then make a spot in the bottom left hand corner of the mount. When the slide is inserted in the projector, the spot should be in the top right-hand corner on the side away from the screen. On plastic mounts the spot can be incorporated by using a self-adhesive label; these and self-adhesive labels for titling purposes, can be obtained at most photographic dealers or stationers.

Transparencies sent by post should be well protected and carefully packed, preferably in the type of box in which slides are returned from the processors. A stamped and self-addressed label should be inserted in the box for the return of your work. As an additional safeguard, write your name, address and title of the slide on the inside of the box.

Alternatively, if you are submitting your entry in an

envelope, the transparency should be inserted in a translucent negative bag and placed between two pieces of rigid cardboard. The translucent bag should be attached to one of the stiffeners with clear adhesive tape for further protection. The idea of placing a cardboard stiffener in the return envelope as suggested for prints, is worth observing.

Keeping Records

Make a note of all photographic competitions you enter. An exercise book is ideal for the purpose. Columns can be drawn up with the following headings: negative number; title of picture; name of competition or publication; date sent; result and date pictures returned, and a final column for any other remarks. By keeping details in this way you can refer to a comprehensive file of all prints and transparencies submitted and have a permanent record of your successes too.

Keep Taking and Making Pictures

To be a contender in the closing stages of a contest, you should strive to produce your best work at all times. Whether you are framing a subject in your viewfinder, deliberating upon which competition to enter, or deciding on the kind of photograph to submit—by observing the foregoing you will provide a sound basis for your competition endeavour.

If you have the aptitude for visualizing and producing a picture, then you should be successful in finding your name amongst the winners. Alternatively, if you feel a lack of ability, do not be discouraged but acquire confidence from a foundation of straightforward methods and ideas, then proceed to something more ambitious.

Photography is both absorbing and enjoyable, entering competitions is an exhilarating extension of the enjoyment and an exciting stimulus to taking and making better pictures.

'Timber and Tiles': The fact that the location is George Washington's Stables, Mount Vernon, U.S.A. would have no influence with a competition judge or a panel or selectors for an exhibition. But it is an example of a style that stands out from conventional architecture photographs mainly because of the repetition in the roof pattern and its austerity in the picture arrangement.
Camera club exhibition award winner.

Rolleiflex T   Ilford FP4   75mm lens   1/125th sec @ f5.6

Where to find Competitions and Exhibitions

Details of photographic contests are announced and made known by magazines, newspapers, manufacturers, tour operators and various organizations.

Apart from other activities, photographic societies and clubs organize competitions and exhibitions and provide splendid opportunities for the aspiring contestant.

Photography magazines frequently publish news of competitions and exhibitions and are an excellent source for obtaining up-to-date information. Also most of the following list of magazines run their own contests, some of them on a regular basis.

'End of the Day': The purpose of the shot was to capture the mood created by the late evening sunlight. Exposure was delayed until the boat penetrated the area of reflection in the water. The prominent highlights are counterbalanced by the dark tone of the quay, which gives strength to an otherwise dull expanse. A further benefit, which became apparent only after the print was developed, is that the quay is of similar length and runs parallel to the line of disturbed water and the boat.

Camera club exhibition award.

Rolleiflex T   Ilford FP4   75mm lens   1/30th sec @ f5.6

Competitions

Amateur Photographer Editor: Barry Monk. Prospect House, 9-13 Ewell Road, Cheam, Surrey, SM1 4QQ.

Camera Weekly Editor: George Hughes. Haymarket Publishing Ltd., 38-42 Hampton Road, Teddington, Middlesex TW11 OJE.

SLR Photography Editor: Barry Hunter, Bushfield House, Orton Centre, Peterborough, Cambs PE2 OUW.

Photography Editor: Nigel Skelsey. Argus Specialist Publications Ltd., 1 Golden Square, London W1R 3AB.

Practical Photography Editor: Dominic Boland. Bushfield House, Orton Centre, Peterborough, Cambs PE2 OUW.

The Photographic Journal Editor: R. H. Mason MA, FBIPP, Hon. FRPS. The Royal Photographic Society, The Octagon, Milsom Street, Bath, Avon BA1 1DN. (*The Photographic Journal* is provided free to all members of the RPS but is available to non-members. Details of cost available from the above address.)

Exhibitions

The following national and international exhibitions are some of the major exhibitions organized each year. Further details of the rules, conditions and dates can be obtained from the organizers at the addresses listed below, which were confirmed as correct at the time of going to press. Always send a stamped and addressed envelope with your enquiry.

Birkenhead Photographic Association International Colour Salon D. G. Cooper, ARPS, APAGB, 29 Fairview Road, Oxton, Birkenhead, L43 5SD.

Bristol International Salon of Photography Fred Matthews ARPS, 229 Luckwell Road, Bristol BS3 3HD.

East of England Show Open Photographic Exhibition East of England Showground, Peterborough PE2 OXE.

Edinburgh P. S. International Exhibition of Pictorial Photography Miss G. L. Alison, Hon. FRPS, 40a, Inverleith Place, Edinburgh EH3 5QB.

Essex International Salon of Photography Cliffs Pavilion, Station Road, Westcliff-on-Sea, Essex SSO 7RA.

Galway C. C. Annual Open Exhibition Michael Kelly, Cong, Co Mayo, Eire.

London Salon of Photography Edwin Appleton, FRPS, 8 Paddock Walk, Warlingham, Surrey CR3 9HW.

Midland Salon of Photography E. H. G. Hodgkiss, ARPS, 55 Thurlston Avenue, Solihull, West Midlands B92 7NZ.

Northern Counties Photographic Federation International Exhibition of Colour Transparencies Mrs. Jane Black, LRPS, 15 Southlands, Tynemouth, Tyne and Wear NE30 2QS.

Nottingham National Open Exhibition of Photography Mrs. B. Michael, ARPS, 'Farleigh', Clifton Lane, Ruddington, Nottingham NG11 6AA.

Paisley International Colour Slide Exhibition Duncan I. McEwan, 'Dunarden', Horsewood Road, Bridge of Weir, PA11 3AT, Scotland

Rushden Open Colour Slide Exhibition G. Smith, 6 Benedict Close, Rushden, Northants NN10 9PH.

Scottish Salon of Photography Rod Wheelans, 'Jensara', Torthorwald, Dumfries DG1 3QA, Scotland.

Smethwick P. S. International Colour Exhibition R. Sills, FRPS, 'Treevale', May Hill, Longhope, Gloucestershire.

Solihull P. S. Open Exhibition of British Photography B. Moore, FRPS, 185 Barn Lane, Olton, Solihull, West Midlands.

Southampton International Exhibition of Photography N. J. Scott, 74 Stannington Crescent, Totton, Hants.

The Royal Photographic Society Annual International Slide Competition and Exhibition. Also *Annual International Print Exhibition.* The Octagon, Milsom Street, Bath, Avon BA1 1DN.

Welsh International Colour Slide Exhibition W. A. Stuart-Jones, ARPS, 52 Caswell Road, Mumbles, Swansea.

Index